Teaching and Using ICT in Secondary Schools

Teaching
and Using ICT in
Secondary
Schools

Terry Russell

David Fulton Publishers
London

David Fulton Publishers Ltd
Ormond House, 26–27 Boswell Street, London WC1N 3JZ

www.fultonpublishers.co.uk

First published in Great Britain in 2001 by David Fulton Publishers

Note: The right of Terry Russell to be identified as the author of this work has been asserted by him in accordance with the Copyright, Designs and Patents Act 1988.

Copyright © 2001 Terry Russell

British Library Cataloguing in Publication Data
A catalogue record for this book is available from the British Library.

ISBN 1–85346–670–0

Typeset by Elite Typesetting Techniques, Eastleigh, Hampshire
Printed in Great Britain by The Cromwell Press Ltd, Trowbridge, Wilts.

Contents

Acknowledgements

There have been many schools involved in the production of this book through the case studies discussed. There is no doubt that much good is happening with ICT in education and I thank them for their involvement in sharing their ideas and practices. I would also like to thank my son Peter for his help with some of the diagrams, Chris Newman and John Hanson for their contributions with the post-16 work, and Brian Appleby, Mark Mendes and Nic Innocent for their help in discussing school-based practices in ICT. I would also like to thank Nick Whittaker for his advice on Internet issues. Finally, I have appreciated the support of my own PGCE IT trainees who have no doubt suffered as I have gone through the data collection process.

Introduction

Information and Communication Technology (ICT) has always been problematic in secondary schools. Prior to the global acceptance that ICT can change just about everything that we do, there was 'just another' curriculum subject entitled Computing Science. There was no thrust to include it in every other subject, no need to include teachers from other subjects, just the Computing Science specialist (who admittedly could have come from another discipline originally) teaching students who had elected to study the subject at either Key Stage (KS) 4 (**General Certificate of Secondary Education: GCSE**) or **Advanced (A) level**. In many ways, the computing specialist had a similar role to the Economics or Business Studies teacher, focusing on a subject after Key Stage 3. This has all changed now: although Computing Science is still available beyond Key Stage 4, ICT has taken over as the subject which should be spanning the complete secondary years in a variety of forms.

It is timely to produce a book which looks at the use of ICT in secondary schools. The use of ICT within most of the established curriculum subjects is on the increase, although this is not universal across the UK. ICT is now a subject of training, vast amounts of finance have been injected into schools through the **New Opportunities Fund (NOF)**, the **National Grid for Learning (NGfL)** and various other initiatives set up through the **British Educational Communications and Technology Agency (BECTA)**, previously the **National Council for Educational Technology (NCET)**. Funding has been available in various guises over the years and has been targeted towards encouraging teachers to include ICT in the delivery of their chosen subject.

This is a practical book; most chapters include examples of what is taking place in schools and can be dipped into at the appropriate place. There is much good practice in schools and it is important that these examples are looked at as well as not so good examples. We often dwell on the problems in education without giving the time to areas of excellence.

This book is written from the perspective of the teacher-practitioner and is aimed at a broad audience of teachers and trainee teachers from the following groups:

- Practising teachers of established National Curriculum subjects who want to integrate ICT into their subject teaching
- Subject-specific ICT teachers who are interested in extending their understanding of the use of ICT across other curriculum subjects
- Trainee ICT teachers who need specific examples of how to apply their subject knowledge across broader curriculum subjects through both the integration of ICT and subject specific applications at Key Stage 4 and beyond
- Teachers who are involved or interested in mentoring ICT trainees throughout the Postgraduate Certificate of Education (PGCE) year. This is an increasingly important aspect of the training process.

Both teachers and trainee teachers are important for this book as they are now tied together through increasing developments and demands of inclusivity put on the teaching profession; the transition from training to full qualification involves practising teachers more than ever.

Structure and rationale

This book has three parts: the origins of ICT and the ICT teacher training process; the organisation and management of ICT; and ICT across the 11–18 age range.

The key objectives of each chapter are stated at the start and where appropriate, practical exercises have been designed to enable you to focus on these objectives with specific reference to your current school experiences. Sometimes you will need to undertake a little research within your own institution to find out key facts and information regarding the topic of the particular chapter. Where possible, the activities have solutions and these are either at the end of the section or are discussed after the appropriate activity, depending on the activity focus. Activities which are in-house do not have solutions because this would be inappropriate.

Data collection

The practical nature of this book can be seen through the various case studies used to exemplify good practice. We all want to move the ICT debate forwards and the best way to do this is to look at what is currently taking place, reflect on it and make decisions as a result of those reflections. Teachers and schools are in the best position to decide how to implement statutory requirements and even if they get it wrong, there will be a foundation provided which can be worked on. The assessment of ICT is a good example of this; many schools which had little in place a few years ago have now developed good ICT auditing and assessment strategies.

As a PGCE **Information Technology (IT)** coordinator, I spend much of my time in schools observing trainee teachers as well as discussing curriculum issues with school mentors. The examples given throughout this book represent live examples of what is happening, collected over a two-year period. As well as the statutory requirements of the secondary key stages, there is also innovation in progress: for example, the use of palmtop computers discussed in Chapter 3, the teaching of interface design issues in Chapter 7 and the on-line art resource used across several key stages discussed in Chapter 9.

Part 1: The origins of ICT and the ICT teacher training process

Even though ICT is a relatively new curriculum subject, the introduction of computers into education dates back to the late 1970s in the case of secondary schools, although the closest link to the use of ICT across the curriculum can be seen a little later with the introduction into primary schools. The nature of the primary curriculum dictates that computers should be used within other subjects, although it must be said that this was not a huge success at the time. Chapter 1 looks at the introductory period of computers in education with a particular focus on the insights and developments which have influenced what is currently happening in schools.

Chapter 2 looks at the teacher training process. Since 1990, secondary teachers have generally been trained through a PGCE programme. These programmes can take either one or two years depending on the institution. Many institutions offer a two-year programme in order to enable graduates from other disciplines to enter the ICT teaching profession and spend the first year of the programme developing their ICT subject knowledge. Also, many institutions are now working on flexible PGCE routes into teaching. Whatever the programme, the teacher training process extends until the end of the induction year. Trainees take a **Career Entry Profile (CEP)** into their first appointment and it is the responsibility of the school to ensure that further training needs are met. Current changes to the teacher training process are discussed in Chapter 2 and these form an integral part to the understanding of educational change; schools share responsibility in the training of teachers and always form the most significant element of a partnership agreement between them and a teacher training or **higher education institution** (HEI); 66 per cent of the training year is spent in schools and school–HEI collaboration now extends to the assessment of trainees through the school mentor. Of course, partnership arrangements vary between institutions but there have never been so many people involved in the training process. Many training programmes now involve school-based mentors teaching various parts of the HEI element of PGCE programmes; the partnership element of training has evolved considerably since the mid-1990s.

Teacher training not only is about conformity, but also has to involve elements of innovation and there is no better subject to look at than ICT. Indeed, ICT teachers need to incorporate innovation into their work all the time, as new technological developments occur.

Part 2: The organisation and management of ICT

Chapter 3 investigates the organisation and management of ICT and links this to current hardware trends and software availability. The organisation and management of ICT are crucial in secondary schools and usually dictate the level of integration of ICT throughout the school. I have discussed examples of good setups which facilitate integration and you will have the opportunity for comparison with your own school situation. Innovative approaches to hardware and organisation (for example, the use of palmtop computers) are investigated as a flexible resource to supplement a larger hardware resource.

Chapter 4 provides the starting point for secondary ICT development through issues related to the primary–secondary transfer. This has always been problematic and through initiatives such as the national numeracy and literacy strategies, there has never been a better time for primary and secondary teachers to communicate and develop their curricula accordingly. The case study used illustrates a good application of a centralised resource along with examples of ICT curriculum organisation and delivery. It is important that secondary **ICT coordinators** are aware of the ICT sophistication that Year 7 students can bring with them and plan accordingly to accommodate their abilities through differentiated programmes.

Part 3: ICT across the 11–18 age range

Chapter 5 provides practical examples of how ICT can be incorporated into other subjects and the examples used are intended to be a starting point for further development. You will be encouraged to explore ICT within other subjects or at least to have an appreciation that the little acorn approach can be effective and provide a new dimension to the teaching of traditional subjects, not to mention the learning experience for the student. All curriculum subjects should be using ICT in an appropriate way, but national inspection findings suggest that this is rather patchy.

An important part of teaching ICT is being able to spot when a student is making an error of conception; the task in hand may be achieved perfectly well, but the process worked through may be laborious and not the most efficient. There are many common ICT misconceptions made by students and Chapter 5 also investigates this.

Various methods of the assessment of ICT capability are investigated in Chapter 6. These are closely linked to the planning of ICT at Key Stage 3 where there is a statutory requirement to report ICT capability.

We accept the **Graphic User Interface (GUI)** that shapes our interaction with the personal computer (PC) but do we understand the meanings given to the icons on the screen? Chapter 7 includes a discussion of GUI design issues taking place in Year 10.

This leads on to issues related to specific ICT teaching at Key Stage 4. This will be of interest to schools where ICT is offered as a Key Stage 4 subject and to those who are now beginning to think about offering it. GCSE is offered in short- and full-course modes and common to both is a coursework element. Specific coursework is looked at and related to one particular examination board syllabus. All GCSE courses have a 60 per cent coursework component.

Chapter 8 continues along the ICT subject knowledge path by looking at post-16 courses and in particular, the A level and **Advanced Vocational Certificate of Education (AVCE)**. Teaching the post-16 age range arguably provides the most difficult task in terms of subject knowledge for the ICT teacher (who may come from a different subject background). This chapter includes some examples of project work suitable for the post-16 syllabuses stated and these provide a route for the development of subject knowledge outside this book.

The use of the Internet has increased dramatically since 1998, particularly for the purposes of research. Chapter 9 looks at a particular resource-based approach to Internet inclusion in the curriculum; although this is located within Art, there are many generic elements to the work and there is no reason why such a resource should not be set up in any curriculum subject. Also, this chapter investigates the use of electronic communication within the Key Stage 3 curriculum and also as a resource for teachers. The distinction is made between electronic mail (email) and conference communication.

The term ICT has recently replaced IT in that it refers to the extra C (Communication) dimension of the technology. Use throughout this book is within the appropriate context; for example, when discussing courses, some are still designated as IT and this has been preserved.

Appendix

In the appendix there is a glossary of terms used in the book, which will be a useful reference section with the many new phrases and acronyms being used in the area of ICT education. This is not meant to be a complete ICT glossary as these are readily available through the web.

PART 1

The origins of ICT and the ICT teacher training process

CHAPTER 1

ICT in education: the historical context

The objectives of this chapter are as follows:

- To investigate relevant background issues to ICT in education with particular reference to how these have informed today's thinking
- To contextualise the growth of ICT in education in the light of technological developments.

If you are in a position to compare good software that you are familiar with to what was available in the early 1990s, then you will probably reflect on some or all of the following:

- today's software is generally easier to use
- yesterday's software had few graphics
- much of today's applications software can be used by most age ranges
- yesterday's software had few help files included with it.

The list is endless. However, you may feel that the following could also be the case:

- some of today's software has its roots in yesterday's software.

It is possible to relate the design of much current software to yesterday through the **generic software elements** associated with both old and new. For example, software that can be placed in categories such as data handling and word processing started school life on early computers such as the BBC micro; although today's software in these categories has many more facilities, the core features are there in both generations. It is worth looking at the background to the current ICT setup in schools in order to get a feel for how developments have taken place.

The 'Micros in Schools' scheme was introduced in the late 1970s, when schools were offered half the funding to buy a microcomputer. The first initiative was for secondary schools and most schools purchased the 380Z from Research Machines Limited (RML). Secondary schools had a head start two years before primary schools and by the time the scheme was extended into primary, the BBC model B had been produced by Acorn; this was the preferred system purchased, with help from the local education authority (LEA), which at the time played an important part in the selection and maintenance of hardware.

Although the introduction of microcomputers into schools was to mean a mismatch of hardware between primary and secondary, this was not a problem at the time because microcomputers were used for different things in different schools. Also, the National Curriculum was not a feature of the process.

Computers across the curriculum

The use of software across the curriculum has its roots firmly anchored in the primary school curriculum, which dictates that there is a subject focus to the use of ICT and this is broadly reflected in the first batch of software available to primary schools. Along with the introduction of micros through the 'Micros in Schools' hardware scheme came the Microprimer package, which consisted of 30 items of software written for primary school use. The secondary 'Micros in Schools' scheme did not contain software because it was not envisaged that the sponsored computer would be used for anything other than a tool for use in Certificate of Secondary Education (CSE) and General Certificate of Education (GCE) Computing Science type subjects (at the time) and in particular, a tool for computer programming in project work. The following two scenarios were typical computing usage in the early 1980s.

The primary scenario: one computer per school with Microprimer software

At the time of the introduction of microcomputers into primary schools, my discussions with head teachers suggested that they were going through a period of trying out, using the supplied hardware and software for a period of time before they developed a strategy for use. The computer of the day was the BBC model B, and was located in either one class each week or one class each term; both structures were tried across the UK and whatever the situation, the lack of hardware made it very difficult to include the computer in the planning and delivery of a learning experience for all pupils. Usage was confined to the Microprimer software supplied and most of the software was of little value. For example, Anag is a simple anagram program that gives a list of words at the top of the screen with some hangman-like dashes underneath. The user has to guess the anagram. Unfortunately, the program will allow only pressing of the correct letters even if there can be more than one anagram. Also, the words are not in any kind of context. Another software item is Trains, a simple drill and practice program for addition. If you get the sum correct, some trains appear on the screen; if you give a wrong answer, some trains disappear, crashing off the screen in what was then spectacular fashion. In other words, there is a more interesting reward for a wrong answer. However, it wasn't all gloom and doom! An example of a better piece of software can be found in Animal, an item of software that has many derivatives today. Animal is a **branching database** that develops a level of intelligence as it is used. It does this by having a question and answer bank that extends as the user types in more questions and answers. A typical branch looks as shown in Figure 1.1. As you will see, it is a well-used program today, albeit in a more sophisticated manner.

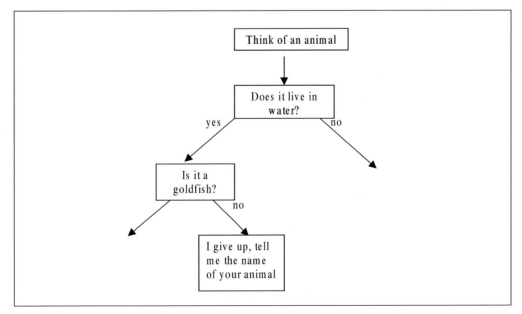

Figure 1.1   Typical branch from the Animal branching database

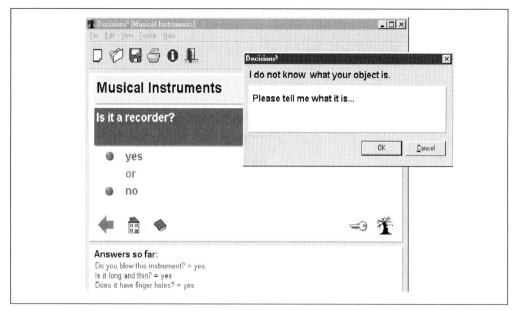

Figure 1.2   Decisions software, generically similar to Animal

So, if the user's animal isn't a goldfish, the answer given then becomes a part of its vocabulary and can be used next time around. The interface was quite primitive in the 1980s but the concept has been extended and developed over the years because it is a worthwhile application. The modern, PC equivalent of this software is entitled Decisions (available from Black Cat Educational Software at www.blackcatsoftware.com), as illustrated in Figure 1.2. You can see the GUI approach which has made the screens more appealing than anything possible on the BBC model B: however, the educational content is very close to the original, encouraging children to adopt **questioning techniques**. Good software can generically survive technological developments and remain relevant. Generically, the ICT keywords associated with Animal and Decisions are branching database, problem solving and questioning techniques and these all form part of the school curriculum; software containing these elements has a good chance of being useful and relevant to the delivery of the National Curriculum.

Activity 1.1
Investigate an item of software in your subject area that is well used. List the generic elements of it that could possibly stand the test of time with successive developments in technology.

The secondary scenario: one computer per school with no curriculum integration

At the time of the introduction, computer usage in the secondary school was limited to a different type of remote access from the one we use at home now. Students studying CSE and GCE Computing Science type subjects had to write programs, usually in **BASIC (Beginners' All-Purpose Symbolic Instruction Code)**, and send the programs to the LEA computer centre for processing. The results would be returned by the following week and the program either would run or would need editing. You can see that this process is rather laborious and quite remote from the user, so the localisation of hardware in school was a good start to further computing developments.

At the time, there was no IT subject in the secondary school; indeed, there were rarely specialist computing teachers either. The responsibility for computing usually fell in the lap of Maths or Science teachers as they may have had an introduction to computing in their initial training. This would have been limited to a little programming so there was a steep learning curve to follow. This approach is, of course, similar to the current scenario in schools where the ICT coordinator may well have come from another discipline although this is now changing (as discussed later).

For secondary schools, the introduction of hardware did not come with a similar range of software, as was the case for primary schools. There were no word processors available for micros and it was not until further funding was injected in the mid-1980s that software became more tailored towards the curriculum; simple word processors for the BBC computer had the appearance of fonts in the way that they would be printed out, a feature known as **WYSIWYG (What You See Is What You Get)**, pronounced Whizzeewig; simple database programs hailed the start of computerised data handling, and information retrieval and graphics programs became available along with simple spreadsheets.

The introduction of the National Curriculum in 1989 heralded the rethinking of the role of IT within schools: IT was now an **Attainment Target (AT)** within Technology but more importantly, IT for all was now a statutory requirement. Of course, if you investigate the way IT was delivered in the early days, you will see that even statutory requirements were not generally met.

Government initiatives and the growth of computers in schools

Most LEAs looked upon the1980s as a pump-priming period for kickstarting the use of computers in schools. If this was the case, then the period of pump priming is surely over, but how would we know? The background to ICT developments has been hugely technology driven and it is clear to see that successive government initiatives came about as a result of a new technology being available. Such initiatives date back to the availability of a floppy disk drive for the BBC computer and more recent ones such as the use of portables for teachers. These initiatives take the form of financial inducement and incentives to extend school resourcing. It is only recently that funding through the New Opportunities Fund has been available with a focus on delivery and not equipment purchasing.

An example of government funding: the background to multimedia in education

All schools use multimedia in some way, through the use of **CD-ROMs (Compact disc read only memory)**, the web or various other multimedia applications. To get to this stage, the background to multimedia in schools is illustrated in Table 1.1.

1986 – 8	Interactive Video in Schools project packages with videodisc, software and materials developed for trialling in 92 schools
1986	Domesday Project: 14,000 schools helped to produce the National Disc (data, text, photos) but used a different system – advanced interactive video (AIV) – from the other interactive video systems
1988	Two interactive video (IV) systems into every LEA and one to every teacher training establishment (BBC or Nimbus systems); many chose the AIV system
1987 – 90	Interactive Video in Further Education: funding for a number of courseware packages plus computers linked to laserdisc players
1990	The National Curriculum Council commissioned two IV discs for primary and three for secondary schools

1993	Funding for a primary and a secondary system to every LEA
1991 – 3	CD-ROM in schools project: drives and discs for 523 secondary, 30 primary and 7 special schools
1994	£4.5 million to put 2,000 complete systems into primary schools
1995	£5 million to put complete systems into secondary schools

Table 1.1   Background to multimedia in schools

There have been similar initiatives for getting schools on-line, further hardware purchasing through various portable schemes and the current scheme of providing 50 per cent of the cost of a computer for eligible teachers. Up-to-date details of initiatives can be found on the BECTA web site at www.becta.org.uk

Taking the view that introducing new technology into schools happens because the technology is there is realistic in the case of multimedia; government schemes of the early 1990s happened when most CD-ROMs were simply text-based applications such as newspaper archives. Indeed, the primary school experience was worse than the secondary one because most primary schools at the time had purchased Acorn hardware and CD-ROMs for this platform were few and far between.

To become included as a CD-ROM supplier through the 1994 scheme, software producers were asked to tender to have their CD-ROMs included in the initiative. Some simply put their current floppy disk based software onto the new medium, hence not using the new speed and space available with CD technology. Some of the CD-ROMs were only 20 per cent full. However, there is no doubt that CD-ROM/multimedia initiatives have benefited through constant development of software, even though many information-based CD-ROMs (for example, Encarta) are now available for use on the web.

If government initiatives have tended to be technology led, then so have our assumptions about the learning experiences of children. All schools now use a GUI, usually a version of Windows. We accept developments such as Windows because we have to, even though there is little research to suggest that it is easier to use a GUI rather than a command-driven interface such as MS-DOS. Maddux (1993) suggests that we hype up technological developments without cause and that through subsequent developments in technology, we assume that the educational experience of the learner is richer. But of course, there is no way of knowing this if we do not research it. There is no automatic educational value in mere exposure to computers. The context of use has to be provided and it is this that makes the use of ICT so interesting.

Summary

In this chapter, I have discussed the background to the rationale behind the expansion of ICT in schools in the context of funding through government initiatives and the 'it is there so let's use it' approach to technological developments. We now have a generic range of software being used in schools and although much of it has advanced facilities, the core elements come from previous generations of software used on the old BBC model B and other hardware.

Much good use has been made of ICT in schools but it is worth reflecting on the reasons for introducing new technologies and the responsibility of teachers to ensure that the best use is made of what is available. Secondary schools have gradually developed from Computing Science as a subject to ICT (some schools offer both at post-16) and to the use of ICT within other subjects. Primary schools introduced computers through the software that was supplied at the time and this has gradually changed through a range of government initiatives that seem to have come thick and fast. There is no doubt that the financial investments over the years are starting to pay off as there is much taking place in schools.

I suggest that we are now past the initial pump-priming stage and should be working towards a position of security, incorporating new technological developments into the planning process as they occur.

Solution to Activity 1.1

There are many possible solutions to this, for example:

- *English*: a spelling program incorporating letter patterns. Spelling is a visual process and words can be represented well in a GUI.
- *Maths*: a program that produces graphs from inputted data. The activity could centre around the interpretation of the graphs and could include the development of higher order skills such as which graph gives the best representation of the data? Is three-dimensional (3D)

representation better than two-dimensional (2D)? Higher order skills in this case refers to the skills being developed and explored as a result of the ICT application.

- *Science*: data logging and the production of graphs for analysis.
- *Modern Foreign Languages (MFL)*: a talking word processor in a target language for speech synthesis in French.

Reference

Maddux, C. (1993) 'Past and future stages in educational computing research', in Waxman, H. and Bright, G. (eds) *Approaches to Research on Teacher Education and Technology*. Charlottesville, Va: Association for the Advancement of Computing in Education.

CHAPTER 2

The partnership between higher education and schools: training ICT teachers

The objectives of this chapter are as follows:

- To discuss recent changes to the structure of secondary ICT teacher training
- To investigate a specific model for a training partnership in ICT
- To discuss elements of school involvement in the training process
- To relate the training process to the induction year.

Having set the background in Chapter 1, it is important to understand how schools can now become involved in the teacher training process. In ICT, the training process produces the ICT coordinators and subject specialists of the future.

Throughout this chapter, I refer to IT (not ICT) trainees because most teacher training courses still use the term. Many will have changed during 2001 and as with all IT/ICT discussions, terminology becomes out of date very quickly even if the content does not.

It is essential that schools are aware of and take part in the training of teachers: training programmes are no longer completely under the control of HEIs and most secondary schools now participate in training. The training process is quite different from what it used to be; the main PGCE route into secondary teaching has two distinct features:

- All training programmes are based on a partnership between HEIs and schools.
- The training process has two distinct elements to it: the training year along with the induction year. In the case of a two-year PGCE programme, the training process is over three years.

It is important that when schools employ newly qualified teachers (NQTs), they are aware of their roles and responsibilities in the second phase of the training process. This chapter will guide you through the training process and involve you in course design issues from a practical perspective.

A trainee teacher needs to come out the other end of a training course as someone who is able to teach. This may sound like a simplistic view of training but it wasn't that long ago that a training course involved little observation of trainees teaching and any structures imposed on trainees were done so locally by the institution in attendance. There were few national standards to achieve, no national body overseeing the process and little consistency in the assessment of trainees. This is not to suggest that all is now fine, but times are certainly changing. With so many agencies involved in the training process it is worth looking at the role of each of them.

The **Teacher Training Agency (TTA)** is responsible for putting into place the standards for the award of **Qualified Teacher Status (QTS)**. The agency works independently from HEIs and any statutory requirement from them has to be incorporated into a training programme, no matter what has been validated internally by the HEI. The TTA works under the guidance of the **Department for Education and Skills (DfES)**, formerly the Department for Education and Employment (DfEE), and is managed by it.

The Office for Standards in Education (OFSTED) has the responsibility for inspecting HEI courses in the same way as it inspects schools: OFSTED measures the criteria laid down in statutory format on a scale of compliance (1 – very good, 2 – good, 3 –adequate), plus 4 – non-compliant. Inspections of Initial Teacher Training (ITT) courses take place over a one-year period, involving several visits looking at different elements of the programme.

The background to the PGCE IT

The PGCE IT is one of the newest PGCEs on offer. It is almost as if we have worked backwards in the training process by realising that the ICT coordinator in school often has a non-specialist qualification and have come to the conclusion that future coordinators need to be trained to do the job. The TTA approved the setting up of PGCE IT courses for the first time in 1996.There are at least 25 providers for ICT teacher training and as mentioned previously, programmes are moving in the same direction as the National Curriculum by beginning to rename them ICT. This brings the training in line with the teaching that a PGCE graduate will undertake.

Getting on to a PGCE IT: the selection process

Secondary PGCE courses are designated as either 11–16 or 11–18 in age phase and the 'bottom line' criterion for taking on a trainee is that they have to have enough 'subject knowledge' at the end of the course to teach across the complete age range. In the case of an 11–18 course (as most of them are), this could involve the teaching of A level IT, Advanced Vocational Certificate of Education or (for debate) A level Computing Science. The computing science issue is an interesting one because typical successful applicants for PGCE courses have a degree in IT or an IT-related area and this will often not involve computing science concepts. For example, it is possible to gain a good IT degree without studying at the depth required in programming to produce an A level Computing Science project.

This point is made even more interesting when you see that there is not a consensus of agreement between HEIs about recruitment qualifications. IT is designated as a shortage subject and along with this comes recruitment problems: designated shortage subjects often have courses which are not full and HEIs are always under pressure to recruit to target, as schools are, and this tends to increase the recruitment of applicants with degrees which are not solely IT based. Many HEIs include the school-based IT mentor in the process of selection and from my discussions with several HEIs this often works well, not just because two heads are better than one but because the school-based mentor is often in a position to look at broader issues to do with teaching ICT in schools.

Including the school mentor in the interview process can further enhance partnership. Of course, not only is recruitment about subject knowledge, but also there is a vast professional selection process and the mentor's role can be very important in this. Interview processes differ but holistic approaches achieve the best results. One HEI has the following structure for selection:

- A pre-interview written task following an observation in a school
- An interview in a partner school conducted by the school mentor
- A presentation and further interview at the HEI (along with the school mentor).

This enables selection to be as thorough as possible.

Teacher training incentives

Since 2000, most trainee teachers have been eligible for a training salary, paid regularly during the training year. The TTA documents this as follows through its web site at http://www.canteach.gov.uk/teaching/fsupport.htm

Training salaries

Eligible postgraduate trainee teachers in England, who are resident in the UK and begin their training on an eligible course after September 2000, will receive a £6,000 training salary – the equivalent of £150 a week while you're training... An additional £4,000 is available for eligible postgraduates teaching mathematics, science, modern foreign languages, design and technology or ICT in England. You can claim this when you have successfully completed your induction and embark on your second year of teaching in a maintained school, provided this is within five years of the start of the first academic year after you achieve QTS. This money isn't a loan. There are no fees to pay back. It's that simple.

This money is paid in instalments over the training year. The £4,000 extra for the shortage subjects will be paid towards the end of the induction year. Once it is widely known that these incentives are in place, it should make a difference to recruitment although this is not evident at the moment.

The PGCE structure and course content

There are a range of standards which all courses have to ensure are met before QTS can be awarded to a trainee and HEIs have to tailor their courses so that they are achieved.

The teaching standards

Circular 4/98 (refers to circular number/year) from the DfEE specifies the teaching standards that have to be achieved by a trainee at the end of the pre-induction year. These standards are extensive and each course has to ensure that they are met through rigorous monitoring procedures. Table 2.1 illustrates a section of the standards. The full document can be downloaded from the web at www.dfee.gov.uk/circular/0498.htm Note that Circular 4/98 is currently being revised.

A. Knowledge and understanding
1. Secondary
Those to be awarded Qualified Teacher Status must, when assessed, demonstrate that they:

i. have a secure knowledge and understanding of the concepts and skills in their specialist subject(s), **at a standard equivalent to degree level to enable them to teach it (them) confidently and accurately at: KS3** for trainees on 7–14 courses; **KS3 and KS4 and, where relevant, post-16** for trainees on 11–16 or 18 courses; and **KS4 and post-16** for trainees on 14–19 courses;

B. Planning, teaching and class management
This section details the standards which all those to be awarded Qualified Teacher Status must demonstrate, when assessed, in each subject that they have been trained to teach.

For primary non-core, non-specialist subjects, trainees being assessed for Qualified Teacher Status must meet the required standards but with the support, if necessary, of a teacher experienced in the subject concerned.

2. Primary and secondary specialist subjects
For all courses, those to be awarded Qualified Teacher Status must, when assessed, demonstrate that they have a secure knowledge and understanding of, and know how and when to apply, in relation to their specialist subject, the teaching and assessment methods specified in the ITT National Curriculum for Information and Communications Technology in Subject Teaching.

4. Primary and secondary for all subjects
Planning
For all courses, those to be awarded Qualified Teacher Status must, when assessed, demonstrate that they:

a. plan their teaching to achieve progression in pupils' learning through:

i. identifying clear teaching objectives and content, appropriate to the subject matter and the pupils being taught, and specifying how these will be taught and assessed;

ii. setting tasks for whole class, individual and group work, including homework, which challenge pupils and ensure high levels of pupil interest;

iii. setting appropriate and demanding expectations for pupils' learning, motivation and presentation of work;

iv. setting clear targets for pupils' learning, building on prior attainment, and ensuring that pupils are aware of the substance and purpose of what they are asked to do;

v. identifying pupils who: have special educational needs, including specific learning difficulties; are very able; are not yet fluent in English; and knowing where to get help in order to give positive and targeted support;

b. provide clear structures for lessons, and for sequences of lessons, in the short, medium and longer term, which maintain pace, motivation and challenge for pupils;

c. make effective use of assessment information on pupils' attainment and progress in their teaching and in planning future lessons and sequences of lessons;

d. plan opportunities to contribute to pupils' personal, spiritual, moral, social and cultural development;

e. where applicable, ensure coverage of the relevant examination syllabuses and National Curriculum programmes of study.

Table 2.1   Extract from DfEE circular 4/98

Activity 2.1
Standard A 1(i) in Table 2.1 relates to the subject specialism of ICT. What would you expect an ICT teacher to be able to teach once graduating from a PGCE IT course? If you could be involved in drawing up a draft teaching programme for an IT NQT, what would it include?

Having carried out Activity 2.1, you will have probably included teaching across other subjects: for example, if you are an English teacher, you may well expect an IT NQT to help teach Year 7 word-processing skills (even though much of this could have been done at Key Stage 2). Of course, an element of the course will involve cross-curricular work but it is important that HEIs do not concentrate solely on this. A PGCE course has to focus primarily on the teaching of ICT skills and concepts as it is a subject in its own right. There can be a tension between what schools expect of IT trainees and the structure of an OFSTED inspection of a course. One recent inspection suggested that the course should teach specific ICT concepts more than focusing on the role of the ICT coordinator. HEIs are aware of this problem and try to address it in several ways: it is important that an ICT specialist is aware of cross-curricular activities just as it is important that an ICT coordinator has an ICT specialism, although this is not always the case. The ICT component to a course needs to relate to what the trainee teaches in school. The following example illustrates a trainee workload on teaching practice.

Mary's placement
Mary is on her second teaching practice in an 11–16 school. She has been given a broad range of experiences across all year groups. Her discussion about her work illustrates that she teaches both discrete ICT and a little ICT integrated within English. This is providing the English teacher with some staff development and she intends to deliver ICT within English herself now. Table 2.2 illustrates the structure of her placement.

Year 7 – Students in Year 7 are banded. Teaching two average classes discrete IT – both classes at present are learning about basic formulas in spreadsheets and how to create graphs. Both groups have some very able students in them and I have had to plan extra work for them. I feel I have built a good relationship with both classes and they are producing a good standard of work. Once they have completed their spreadsheets and charts they will be doing a step-by-step evaluation of what they have done.

Teaching the lowest banded Year 7 group with 19 students. This is a very difficult class and I have given them a project which is to produce a front and back cover to their favourite book. Students will draw a picture in Paint which will then be put into Publisher where they will design the front cover. Students will then research what sort of things are on the back covers of books and then create their own. At the end of this they will be doing an evaluation on a worksheet which has been designed appropriate to their needs. I feel that I have developed a very good relationship with this very challenging class and am pleased with the progress they are making.

I am also teaching a Year 7 group cross-curricular English – I am finding this very interesting and really enjoying it. So far I have been working with them on writing a professional letter, searching the Internet for research on their English projects and currently they are creating a newspaper article on their project in Word and Publisher.

Year 8 – I teach two classes of mixed ability. At present we are working on databases. The students have created their own Music databases the information for which they have got from home collections. They have created their databases and are now starting to undertake simple searches. Again, having completed their database I will ask them to do a step-by-step guide (in Word or Publisher) on how they did it including screen dumps from Access.

Year 9 – Two classes of discrete IT and a further English class. The IT students are working on a project to produce incoming and outgoing finances for a fictitious business of their choice. They have first completed weekly incomings in Excel and are at present working on monthly incomings. Following this they will be looking at monthly outgoings, what they might be, and producing a spreadsheet. They will then be working out the monthly profit/loss for their business. Students are learning a range of different formulas to use in Excel. They will also go on to put this information in chart format and will be encouraged to make the choice of chart themselves. They will be aware that the chart(s) they select should be selected as to best show the information and will be asked to justify their choices in an evaluation.

Cross curricular English – I am working with them researching on the Internet and also producing write-ups on *Twelfth Night* – the different characters and their status in the play.

Year 10 – Year 10 GCSE who had been given their projects when I started to teach them. The project is that they were given four choices of business to start up in the local area and to undertake research. They are producing databases for their business and developing at least six queries for their database table. Students have realised errors in their databases when they created queries that won't work. They then have to work out why the query did not work and make amendments to their table. They will go on to undertake mail merges, evaluate their work and complete a test. They must also produce a data capture sheet relevant to their particular business.

Year 11 – GCSE (Full Paper). I am working on their major project with them. Class of 12 students. At present working with them on formulas in spreadsheets working out costings for business sales and also stock control. Also involved in marking minor projects. I will soon be working with them on exporting work from Excel into Access, producing dynamic contents pages in Word. I am working with half of the class individually going through their projects with them and moving them forward.

Table 2.2   Content of Mary's placement

Activity 2.2
Having read Mary's teaching load, suggest ways in which the school ICT mentor could help her in the development of her own subject knowledge.

Teaching practice assessment
Evidence gathering forms a major part of a training course and one way to ensure the standards are met is to set up a triangulation process where the school mentor, HEI tutor and trainee all have their say through the careful documentation of achievement. When trainees are on teaching practice, they have regular observations from the mentor and written feedback constitutes evidence related to a standard (or several standards). One written feedback does not suggest compliance but can be part of a range of evidences. The trainee can then map the standard to the written observations, claiming that this can form a part of the evidence. Daily written observations form a part of the school-based assessment process; all courses have an assessment booklet where students receive summative feedback on a school placement and again, this can form a part of the evidence-gathering process. Finally, the HEI tutor can also undertake observations and this is usually done from the perspective of moderation,

feeding back to the school mentor in areas of consistency of assessment. The HEI tutor is usually in a position to have a holistic view of assessment since he or she will visit a range of schools during the course of a teaching practice. Many HEI tutors undertake paired observations with the school mentor and this again aids the accuracy of assessment.

Some HEIs have set up an Advisory Mentor Scheme where school mentors visit other schools for paired observations with other school mentors. In my experience, this process raises many new issues to aid course development and enables school mentors to gain a broader perspective on their own professional development.

A sample lesson planning format
Crucial to a successful training experience is the planning structure laid down by the training course: trainees (and qualified teachers) need to show that they can clearly distinguish between ICT skills and concepts and that they can build upon the prior experiences and expertise of students. To these ends, Table 2.3 exemplifies a typical lesson planning structure used; this structure was developed between an HEI and several partner schools.

Lesson No. 2	Subject/Topic	ICT/English
	Date	01 Dec 2000
	Time	Lesson 7 (35 minutes)

Points from previous lessons
All students should be at a suitable place to start this piece of work. Remember slower students need write only two paragraphs and use only a few of their sentences.

LEARNING OBJECTIVES
- To understand that a paragraph is a group of related sentences.
- To know what an adjective is and give examples.
- To be able to centre and underline a heading.

> English National Curriculum writing 2b

DIFFERENTIATION
- Able students will use the thesaurus to change some of their adjectives.
- Less able students should aim to complete one paragraph.

PREPARATION
Check students' folders so far.

> Keywords:
> spellchecker, print preview, cut and paste, thesaurus, adjective

ORGANISATION
- Students to sit as per seating plan.

INTRODUCTION
(5–10 minutes)
- Changing sentences into paragraphs. **REMIND** pupils of two spaces after full stop, one after comma and line after paragraph.
- Can use cut and paste to reorder sentences – **EXPLAIN HOW TO USE CUT AND PASTE.**
- Centre and underline the **TITLE.**
- Before printing out (probably won't be this week in most cases) make sure there are plenty of descriptions and remind them of **PROOF READ, SPELLCHECKED AND PRINT PREVIEWED.**
- Use of **ADJECTIVES**, give/ask for examples.

DEVELOPMENT
(20 minutes)
- Students will continue with their writing of paragraphs.
- Once they have checked them they should print them out.
- During this time I will attend to individual questions. Any common questions will be addressed to the class as a whole.

CONCLUSION
- **STOP** class 5 minutes before the end of the lesson and make sure all pupils print off work and put it in their folders.
- Get pupils to fill in their **TASK SHEETS.**
- Recap what has been learnt this lesson.
- Dismiss class and collect folders as students leave.

ASSESSMENT
- Pupils tick on sheet in their folders once they have completed the task.
- Making a mental note of how students are progressing.

Table 2.3   Sample lesson plan, Year 7 ICT and English, Sunnymead School

There are several key issues related to this lesson plan and it is useful to place these issues in the context of the school structure for ICT at Sunnymead School.

Lesson planning issues: Sunnymead School

- In Year 7, ICT is delivered in a cross-curricular way: this lesson is entitled ICT and English as there are elements of both in it. The trainee is expected to have an understanding of the English curriculum, as briefly shown through a National Curriculum reference. The trainee has linked the lesson to the previous one through 'points from previous lesson'.
- Keywords provide the ICT and English subject knowledge focus for questioning and assessment and this also helps the lesson evaluation afterwards
- The trainee has planned work for different abilities within an English context and mentions the drafting facilities inherent in a word-processing application
- The English teacher would normally take this class, not the ICT teacher
- The name of the software is not mentioned
- Individual lesson plans are developed from broader schemes of work.

Activity 2.3
How does the structure in Table 2.3 compare with yours? Discuss the bulleted points with a colleague from the English department.

The ICT Audit
All trainees (not only IT trainees) are now required to collect evidence that they have integrated ICT within their own subject through an audit procedure. The standards document for this is Annex B of Circular 4/98 and Table 2.4 illustrates an extract from this.

---

13. Trainees must demonstrate in relation to the subject and age(s) of pupils to be taught that they:

a. *know how to use ICT to find things out, including, as appropriate for the subjects and the age of pupils to be taught:*

     i. identifying sources of information and discriminating between them; — *e.g. disk, CD-ROM, Internet; up-to-date information from a weather station; low status sources on the Internet with no editorial scrutiny; CD-ROM information which has been through some editorial scrutiny but may be out of date;*

     ii. planning and putting together a search strategy, including framing useful questions, widening and narrowing down searches; — *e.g. translating enquiries expressed in ordinary language into forms required by the system;*

     iii how to search for information, including using key words and strings and logical operators such as AND, OR and NOT, indexes and directories; — *e.g. in searching a database or employing an Internet search engine;*

     iv. collecting and structuring data and storing it for later retrieval, interpretation and correction;

     v. interpreting what is retrieved;

     vi. considering validity, reliability and reasonableness of outcomes; — *e.g. knowing the probable outcome of a calculation rather than just relying on the calculator;*

Table 2.4   Extract from the ICT Standards

For the school recruiting an NQT this appears to be an exciting development in teacher training, and so it is. Recruiting NQTs with an ICT capability in their subject should ensure that the profession is being stocked with ICT literate professionals but there are problems along the way: the main problem lies in the time and resourcing available to collect the necessary evidence. Of course, a second problem for non-ICT trainees is the school's ability to offer ICT within other subjects and this is variable across the UK. Think about 13a(iii) in Table 2.4. Trainees in non-ICT-based subjects do not always have access to the web while on teaching practice and to use a database would involve booking a computer room. It is important that all trainee teachers have access to ICT facilities during the teaching practice component of their course.

HEIs interpret the ICT audit in different ways but most expect trainees to develop a portfolio. Evidence is gathered from as many sources as possible to show ICT development.

PGCE IT course structure: Middlesex University

This case study illustrates a particular HEI's PGCE programme. The structure of the PGCE IT consists of three elements: main subject studies, professional studies and school experience. The structure of each term is illustrated in Figure 2.1.

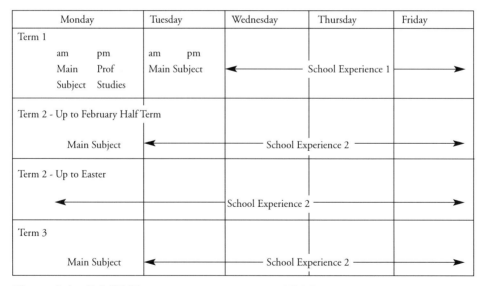

Figure 2.1   PGCE IT programme structure at Middlesex University

School experience
You can see from the structure of this course that school experience is serial: that is, it is continuous throughout the entire course. Not all HEIs operate in this way (for example, some have blocks at the HEI and blocks

in school) but Middlesex has found it a useful model, mainly because the school-based element informs the rest of the HEI-based element: at the start of each week there is a time for reflection and feedback on the previous week. The statutory requirement is that trainees spend 120 days in school over the course of the PGCE.

Mentors are fully involved in the assessment of trainees not just in their own school, but also in others through an Advisory Mentor Scheme which encourages them to undertake paired observations in other local schools. This has enabled a network on mentors to have professional contact on a regular basis. One Advisory Mentor suggests the following:

> Visiting other schools to observe trainees is an excellent way to find out what others are doing. Pairing up with another ICT mentor, observing a lesson together has enabled me to sharpen my own practices and get new ideas about running my department. There just doesn't seem to be the time to reflect on what others are doing and taking part in the training process has enabled me to do this. I have also enjoyed taking part in teaching some elements of the course at the University. I feel fully involved in the process.
>
> (Nic, Advisory Mentor)

Electronic communication with mentors and trainees
All mentors have regular electronic communication through a standard email facility, together with an address list of other mentors in the partnership. The course tutor has also set up a PGCE conference using Yahoo! Groups; this is essentially a web-based bulletin board where mentors can collect course details such as the handbook and all other course documentation. The structure of Yahoo! Groups is discussed in Chapter 9.

All trainees are expected to submit their written work electronically. The work is emailed to the course tutor, marked using the reviewing tool in Word, and emailed back to the trainee. Work such as this can contribute significantly to the ICT audit discussed previously. Although the audit shouldn't be viewed as a tick list, it is nevertheless important for it to be a prominent feature of the PGCE year from day one.

Main subject studies
All PGCE courses have a subject-specific element which distinguishes them from other strands: IT trainees have various subject-specific

elements to work on and this takes the form of a portfolio. The purpose of the portfolio is to illustrate individual subject knowledge development and to ensure that they are able to teach across the complete designated age range of 11–18. Of course, there is some freedom to illustrate subject knowledge development but in itself, this would not guarantee specific skills, knowledge and understanding of the 11–18 requirements of schools. There are laid down assessments which all ICT trainees have to do and all tasks relate subject knowledge to classroom activities and application. The following is a selection of tasks which trainees are required to do.

Task 1: Key Stage 2/3 progression – the link between your current placement and the feeder primary schools
You have all spent time investigating the structure of IT in primary schools through your pre-course experience, as documented in your reflective journal. Having now gained considerable teaching experience in secondary schools, your new task is to investigate the differences between teaching in primary and secondary schools through a structured period of one day (or two half-days) in a primary feeder school.

You need to arrange to undertake the activity specified below. The timings for this are for you to negotiate with your mentor.

You are to spend one day (or two half-days) in a feeder primary school to your current placement. The purpose of this is two-fold:

- To investigate the structure of ICT delivery at Key Stage 2
- To suggest ways to ensure that the transition (in ICT) from Key Stage 2 to Key Stage 3 for students is as smooth as possible. This involves you developing an auditing procedure following discussions with your mentor.

To this end, you are to spend the first half of the day researching under the following headings:

- The delivery of ICT at Key Stage 2
- The responsibility for ICT in the school
- The monitoring, assessment, recording and reporting of ICT capability in the school
- The contact between the primary and secondary school regarding ICT capability and
- The place of ICT in the broader curriculum compared to your experiences at Key Stage 3.

You need to appreciate that it may not be possible to find time for discussions with the ICT coordinator and may decide that the first half-day is spent observing/information gathering in several classrooms.

The second half of the day will involve you observing in a Year 6 class where ICT is taking place. This may involve observation of groupwork or whatever application is taking place. You are to use the standard lesson observation form for this activity.

You are to include the entry in your main subject folder under the heading **Key Stage 2 ICT.** Your entry should have the five headings stated above as well as the auditing procedure that you have designed, and a concluding section with your lesson evaluation clearly filled in. This should include your summative comments regarding the experience.

Rationale

The assessment and development of ICT capability upon entry into the secondary school has been consistently weak and this is illustrated through OFSTED inspections. By mapping ICT skills on entry, teachers have a better chance to develop them further from Year 7 on. There needs to be a strong link between Key Stages 2 and 3.

Task 2: Monitoring, assessment, recording and reporting

Assessment should be one of the key activities undertaken on teaching placement. Formative assessment should take place during each lesson; you should keep records of students' achievement and give regular written feedback on student work. You are to include evidence of your student record keeping and assessment within this stated section. You should write up the section giving details, with examples, of all aspects of your assessment, recording and reporting structure. You should obviously integrate the school structure as much as possible but if ICT assessment on your placement is not detailed, then you will have to develop your own structure. In many ways, this is an ongoing exercise anyway because you have to have this section available, under continuous development, in your main subject file from the start of the programme.

Rationale

Monitoring, assessment, recording and reporting (MARR) are consistently poor in secondary ICT, as stated in many OFSTED inspections. By including an assignment which has MARR up front in the minds of the trainees, there has been more opportunities for them to assess students' work on a regular basis.

Task 3: Logo

You have been introduced to MSW Logo during the course of the previous subject module and have provided evidence of undertaking the work developed during the session given. You now have to think about applications of Logo at either Key Stage 3 or 4. Your task can involve either the teaching of Logo (within a stated context) or the development of a Microworld for use within another subject. You will need to negotiate the teaching within your placement and the length of this aspect of the assignment will depend on your school. Your assessment will take place with regard to the following criteria:

- An introductory paragraph describing the context of the Logo teaching, National Curriculum references, objectives
- Lesson plans, resources for each lesson, e.g. transparencies, user guides and worksheets (with answers)
- Lesson evaluations and an overall summary of achievements, backed up with given feedback (clearly identifiable) to students; this should include common Logo misconceptions if appropriate.

Again, there is a Logo section in your main subject file so this is for development as the programme progresses.

Rationale

There has been considerable debate about the skills needed by trainees to be able to teach ICT effectively: do IT trainees need to program? Do they need to teach Computing Science? By undertaking structured exercises in Logo and ensuring that they teach it in school, there is at least one programming element involved in the course and Logo has been chosen because of its strong cross-curricular links to Mathematics. Their backgrounds are so varied that structured programming is often new to them. An example of the use of MSW Logo is given in Chapter 5.

Task 4: The negotiated task

This task involves you in preparing, teaching and evaluating a teaching package. The booklet that you produce will contain the following sections:

- A title page
- An abstract
- A reference section relating to how the package fits in with the secondary school structure

- The lesson plans and lesson evaluations associated with the package
- A summative evaluation of the package in the context of delivery.

There are, of course, many possibilities for this negotiated task and the following gives you some ideas:

- The setting up of web pages within a stated context
- Developing a **Computer Aided Learning (CAL)** package in Visual Basic for a stated area of the curriculum
- Authoring a multimedia application in Modern Foreign Languages (MFL) or Maths, in conjunction with another trainee.

Rationale

There has to be some flexibility in any assessment and this gives trainees the opportunity to work on a project with the school. Often, the product is left in the school at the end of the placement and is jointly specified by the trainee and the mentor.

General Professional Studies

There is a generic element to teaching and all PGCE courses have a time when trainees from all subjects get together for mass lectures which are followed up with written tasks. This is achieved through **General Professional Studies (GPS)**. A GPS programme will include elements of Classroom Management, Teaching and Learning Strategies, Assessment, Equal Opportunities, Special Educational Needs and the like. The Middlesex programme delivers such generic elements through a mass lecture to trainees from all strands and these are then followed up in the subject strands, where they are related to the subject specialism. A typical Autumn term for GPS looks like this:

Week
1. Reflections on Pre-course Experience
2. Introductory Lecture
3. Classroom Management
4. Teaching and Learning Strategies
5. Assessment
6. Identifying Needs and Setting Targets
7. Equal Opportunities
8. Special Educational Needs
9. Pastoral System and Moral Framework
10. Bullying and Abuse

11. 14–19 Curriculum Developments
12. Visit to School 2
13. Looking Back, Looking Forward

There are seven assessments associated with these sessions and each has a focus within the particular PGCE subject, in this case IT. The assessment for week 5 (i.e. when Assessment is the title of the mass lecture) is as follows:

Assignment 3
Write a reflective account of the importance of ICT assessment issues related to teaching with particular regard to:

• providing evidence of the way in which your lesson planning, teaching and evaluation links to your school and department assessment policies; this should include examples of your planning where appropriate
• how you are planning to maintain evidence of the ongoing marking of pupils' work
• providing evidence of the understanding and consideration of the use of different types of ICT assessment.

This assignment takes the form of an essay with lesson planning examples. The assessment of ICT is central to the PGCE programme and this assignment links with the formative main subject assessment which is ongoing during the second placement. The GPS element of the programme enables trainees from different subjects to mix and discuss ideas common to teaching.

Skills tests

All trainees have to pass three externally set tests in numeracy, literacy and ICT. There are test centres throughout the UK and it is the trainee's responsibility to ensure that these are sat and passed before the end of the training year; this is essential because QTS cannot be awarded until these tests are passed. Currently, trainees have an unlimited number of attempts at the tests. There has been much discussion about the appropriateness of the tests and it is important that trainees have support from both the HEI and school in ensuring they achieve success. Many programmes have arranged extra sessions in these areas in what is already a crowded timetable.

The Career Entry Profile

All NQTs bring the CEP with them into their first teaching post. It consists of various strengths and weaknesses, as highlighted by the trainee. The weaknesses are more to do with areas for further development, even though QTS has been awarded. It is important that the employing school has read the document thoroughly before the start of the induction year as there are induction year training implications for the school. Table 2.5 illustrates a trainee's self-evaluation with the points he will need to work on in the induction year.

Areas in which the Standards for the Award of QTS have been met but where the trainee teacher will benefit from further development during the induction period.

Assessment

1. I feel I have a particular need to develop my understanding of the transition between primary and secondary schools with regard to my specialist subject.

2. I also feel I need to develop my skills regarding the understanding and knowledge of how national, local, comparative and school data, including National Curriculum test data, can be used to set clear targets for pupils, achievement.

Subject knowledge

3. I feel that, considering the rapid development of IT, I will need to constantly update my subject knowledge. In particular this should be focused on areas such as the use of Multimedia presentation software and Internet applications and web page design software.

Teacher's role

4. I feel I need to develop my knowledge of how my specialist subject can help students with learning, emotional and behavioural difficulties.

Table 2.5   Extract from an NQT's Career Entry Profile

As can be seen from the CEP, the NQT has several points to work on. It is important that the school is aware of its role and responsibility in giving this NQT access to the resources necessary to develop in the areas stated in the CEP. Taking the example from Table 2.5, how would you address these NQT needs? Here are some possible solutions.

1. I feel I have a particular need to develop my understanding of the transition between primary and secondary schools with regard to my specialist subject

I think that we all share this problem to some extent. It has already been mentioned that training courses have to focus on the transition from primary to secondary and even though this has been a stated part of the course discussed, it is still seen by this NQT (and others) as a weakness. Links between the two are becoming stronger with numeracy and literacy developments and a starting point for this trainee could be to become involved in the liaison work that all secondary schools do. The NQT needs to visit primary schools, look at the ICT provision, encourage workshops held at the secondary school for Year 6 students. Also, a Year 7 ICT provision should make reference to prior learning and so the NQT could be part of an audit process at the beginning of Year 7.

2. I also feel I need to develop my skills regarding the understanding and knowledge of how national, local, comparative and school data, including National Curriculum test data, can be used to set clear targets for pupils' achievement

It is important that an NQT can visit other schools, both locally and further afield. The setting of individual targets is part of a tricky process and needs to be done after the gathering of information from a range of sources. Do we set regular targets for students? If we do, how are they monitored? Are they realistic? And (more importantly) have they already been achieved in the primary school? An NQT should be able to interact with other NQTs locally, at least, and this could aid the development of these skills.

3. I feel that, considering the rapid development of IT, I will need to constantly update my subject knowledge. In particular this should be focused on areas such as the use of Multimedia presentation software and Internet applications and web page design software

Subject knowledge is always an issue in a subject that is constantly changing and this does not affect only NQTs. It is important that an NQT has access to resources that facilitate subject knowledge development and this can happen through attending courses and having time to become familiar with new software and the more academic side to courses and in particular the post-16 range offered in the school. If the NQT has finished an 11–18 course then there should have been a reasonable amount of teaching at post-16 level but unfortunately, this may not have been the case through placement circumstances. The CEP should be looked at as a vehicle to improve the provision within the school by facilitating NQT development as stated in the document; the software mentioned in the CEP is not expensive to buy and if the school is not using web page design software then this could be an opportunity for a new ICT initiative following an NQT.

4. I feel I need to develop my knowledge of how my specialist subject can help students with learning, emotional and behavioural difficulties

This could offer an opportunity for the NQT to work with the special educational needs coordinator (SENCO) and again, there could be an opportunity for the SENCO to develop an ICT/SEN (special educational needs) capability that may not have been previously there. The NQT should observe any work currently taking place and be pointed in the direction of an exemplary school nearby, if there is one.

Underlying the above is the slightly reduced teaching load timetabled for an NQT during the induction year. It is essential that a monitoring and recording mechanism is in place so that the NQT can feedback on the self-set targets contained in the CEP. Indeed it may be necessary to modify them if they are not appropriate.

Activity 2.4
At some stage during the year, there will need to be observations of the NQT in the teaching situation. List the headings that you feel should be commented on during an observation. Design an observation sheet.

Summary

In this chapter, I have discussed recent changes made to teacher training programmes and in particular, the structure and content of a particular PGCE programme. Many schools now take part in the teacher training process through various partnerships they have with HEIs and since approximately 66 per cent of a teacher training programme is based in school, the role of the school is key to success for trainees. Teaching practice for IT trainees should involve teaching the subject ICT as well as some work across the curriculum, depending on the way it is delivered in the school. The training process now extends to the induction year and schools need to ensure that they can continue the professional development of the NQT as documented in the CEP.

Solutions to activities

Activity 2.1

Although most PGCE IT trainees have a degree with IT as a major component, there may well be gaps in their subject knowledge, particularly if they have studied a modular degree. Most courses have a subject knowledge auditing procedure where trainees show that by the end of the training year, they can teach up to A level. This is realistic since most secondary PGCE IT graduates have been trained through an 11–18 course and so you should expect them to be able to teach up to A level ICT.

There is currently much debate about whether courses should equip trainees for teaching Computing Science so it would have to be a discussion point with the NQT. An NQT should be able to teach all ICT components taught discretely at Key Stages 3 and 4 as well as ICT across other subjects. As Vocational Certificates of Education (VCEs) are developed, an NQT needs to be flexible to teach new courses which were not there during the training year. It is important that NQTs have a time to adjust from the training year and they should not have too much responsibility, even if it looks as though they can take it. Some IT NQTs have a second subject through their first degree (for example, Business Studies) and this shouldn't be overlooked when arranging a teaching programme.

Activity 2.2

Mentors have a responsibility for trainee subject knowledge development. Mary's teaching programme involves using a range of software so she needs access to software so that she can produce teaching material. Also, the mentor needs to work with her on the GCSE full course project work because she will be unfamiliar with some of the assessments. Subject knowledge development involves the teaching of the subject as well as a personal understanding of the subject matter.

Activity 2.3

The solution to this activity will be dependent upon the setup in your school. A discussion with the English department should centre around the use of ICT within English. Is there any? Who delivers it? What is the context of the delivery?

Activity 2.4

When observing an NQT, the criteria for a good lesson should include the following:

- the depth of planning as illustrated through a lesson plan and how it links to previous and future planning
- issues of teaching and classroom management
- communication skills
- formative and summative assessment through differentiated activities
- the teacher's role
- subject knowledge and application.

Observing NQTs should involve written feedback.

PART 2

The organisation and management of ICT

CHAPTER 3

Hardware, software and the coordination of ICT

The objectives of this chapter are as follows:

- To investigate the responsibility issues for ICT across the school
- To describe specific examples of hardware and software organisation
- To investigate innovative features of hardware and software purchasing (for example, the use of palmtop computers).

Schools' hardware and software resourcing vary considerably across the UK. But it is not just a case of the amount of hardware and software in schools that dictates how the equipment is used: it is possible for a good teacher to use out-of-date hardware more effectively than a not-so-good teacher having access to state-of-the-art equipment. The same is true of software. Organisation and management of ICT resourcing are crucial to the smooth running of ICT both as a subject in its own right and as a tool across other curriculum subjects.

Because the role of ICT within the school is so diverse, it may be that you are not aware of overall responsibility within your school. However, there will be a colleague with the role of ICT coordinator and it is important that you are aware of the roles and responsibilities of this person.

The ICT coordinator: background, roles and responsibilities

NCET (1998) suggested that most ICT coordinators in secondary schools are expected to carry out:

- resource allocation
- system maintenance

- coordination and monitoring of IT usage across the National Curriculum
- staff training
- classroom support for staff.

The ICT coordinator often has other responsibilities within ICT as a subject in its own right. These two distinct roles as coordinator and subject specialist come with broad responsibilities, as illustrated in Figure 3.1.

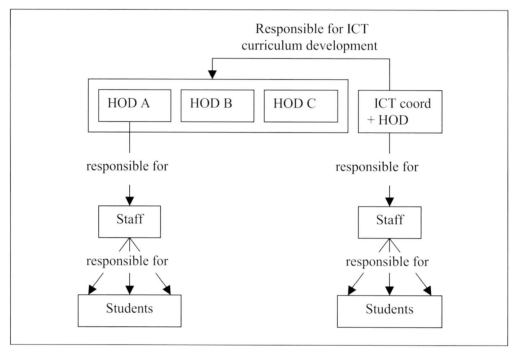

Figure 3.1   Responsibilities and influences of the ICT coordinator

You can see that potentially, the ICT coordinator has more influence on the learning process than any other department. This is more the case when the responsibility line for ICT coordination covers all other departments.

Of course, the responsibilities illustrated in Figure 3.1 do not pertain to all ICT coordinators: the ICT coordinator may not be an ICT specialist, may not teach ICT as a discrete subject and may not be a head of department (HOD). Here are some scenarios for the role and general day-to-day work of the coordinator in two schools chosen from different geographical locations.

School A
School A has an ICT coordinator, who is responsible for teaching ICT across Key Stage 3 along with a colleague from another department. They are both responsible for the assessment of ICT across both key stages (the school is 11–16) and the coordinator teaches the entire GCSE ICT full course. Assessment at Key Stage 3 is through a project set by him without the involvement of other departments. He is an Art specialist who has moved into ICT from an initial interest in ICT within Art. The ICT coordinator generally deals with technical problems although there is a part-time technician for half of the school week. He comments on his daily routine:

> I really enjoy my job but find that I do need another ICT colleague to work with on a full-time basis. It's fine working with John but he is part of the senior management and always has other duties to perform. We need to raise the profile of ICT within the school and this could be initiated by having another member of staff; at least that would make me a department!

This situation exists in many schools. In this case, the school is now looking to make an NQT appointment in ICT. Staff training has ensured that some departments are beginning to use ICT within their subject thus releasing some of the pressure from the ICT coordinator. He feels that even though staff are becoming more ICT literate, he still cannot expect them to be fully responsible for ICT assessment.

School B
School B has an ICT coordinator who is not the head of ICT. She has a responsibility for managing ICT throughout the school within other subjects. Inevitably, there is a staff development responsibility alongside this. The head of ICT is responsible for the subject ICT (i.e. GCSE ICT and Advanced **General National Vocational Qualification (GNVQ) in** this case) but does not have a responsibility for ICT at Key Stage 3, where the bulk of the coordination role is focused. There is also a full-time technician in the school and she is responsible for the setting up and maintenance of hardware. The head of ICT has a degree in Computing Science and the ICT coordinator is a History graduate. The ICT coordinator has the following views:

I do not look upon my job as teaching a subject; all the work I do in other departments has a subject focus in the first instance, then, ICT becomes a part of it. My own development is, more or less, becoming familiar with new packages. The English department recently wanted to use ICT within their project, which involves children writing a letter and mail merging it to send out to local shops. The information was collected and entered into Access and I didn't know how to produce individual letters for the shops. It wasn't hard though but this shows how our school works. The English department could do it themselves really, they just need access to the hardware and a small input from me regarding the ICT bit.

School B has a broader approach to ICT than School A: the differentiated role approach of School B, through viewing the management of ICT as a subject being distinct from using ICT across the curriculum, ensures that the staff see ICT as a subject in its own right. School B has interpreted the term 'coordinator' as a colleague working with staff across a range of subjects, whereas the head of ICT has the same status as the head of Maths, English or Science, that of being responsible for a subject. School B also expects all new appointments to have an ICT capability and this is explored at interview.

Both ICT coordinators mentioned above originally come from a non-ICT background and moved into ICT at a time when there were clear demands on schools to use ICT in the many ways discussed throughout this book. It must be appreciated that it is only recently that specific ICT training courses have been set up by HEIs so ICT coordinators who have been in post for four years or more and have a non-specialist background have had to work through a steep learning curve.

Profiles of three current ICT coordinators
1. A degree and PGCE in Art, four years' Art teaching followed by some ICT teaching through interest and a lack of staff. He now teaches GCSE ICT plus a little Art. ICT is now integrated throughout the Art department and is beginning to be used across other departments. Even though the school is 11–18, there is no ICT post-16.
2. A degree and PGCE in History followed by History teaching for seven years, along with teaching Maths, another shortage subject. ICT was gradually introduced into the school through the Maths Department and she became the first ICT coordinator in the school.

3. A degree in Business Studies followed by a PGCE in Information Technology and two years' teaching experience.

Teacher 3 is in a minority from the discussion above but it is clear to see that a specialist ICT teacher has a clear pathway through a school. Teacher 3 is in a qualified position to establish ICT as a subject in its own right and depending on the type of training received, could develop ICT across other subjects.

The role of the ICT coordinator is often unclear: along with the curriculum responsibility usually comes a hardware and software responsibility and there are many issues to consider to ensure that the cross-school coordination role is undertaken as efficiently as possible.

The organisation and purchase of hardware

Most schools have ICT hardware organised along similar lines through the use of dedicated ICT suites. Along with this may come a range of subsidiary setups where hardware is dispersed across the school. The following case studies give a flavour of the setup in two schools.

Hardware resourcing: Grange Park School
Grange Park School has 132 networked computers. All pupils and staff have their own work areas and email addresses on this network. Microsoft Office 2000 is the main application available on the network. The school recently upgraded from Office 97 and this was useful because Office 2000 includes Publisher, which is used across most curriculum subjects.

There are five dedicated computer rooms. All rooms have one ink-jet and one laser printer. There are some additional computers dispersed throughout the school in dedicated areas such as Design and Technology (used for control), Science (used for data logging) and Art, where there are some Apple Macintosh systems. There is a tradition of Apple hardware in the Art department although future purchases will be PCs because the software is now the same.

There are a range of laptops available for staff to borrow if they wish to give PowerPoint presentations. These are used mainly in the sixth form centre. Along with these laptops comes a liquid crystal tablet for projection using a powerful overhead projector.

There are a range of digital cameras available for use by staff and the school intends to purchase several more as the price comes down. These have recently been used on a field trip, along with the laptop computers. The photographs were transferred to the laptops and incorporated into the write-up of the field trip.

The networked computers have access to the web through the LEA provision.

Rationale

You can see that at Grange Park, there is a centralised approach through the single network of 132 PCs but that there is a dispersement of hardware in other areas such as Science and Art. The use of laptops has several advantages, which are discussed later. Digital cameras are relatively cheap and easy to use and enable you to incorporate photographs into documents.

The central resource is networked and there are several hardware configurations which can be used in a network. All networks require a server and a tried and tested configuration involves the server holding the work areas for users but the applications software being installed on individual members of the network. This way, if you want to access your work, it doesn't matter which computer you log onto. The setup for each dedicated computer room at Grange Park is illustrated in Figure 3.2.

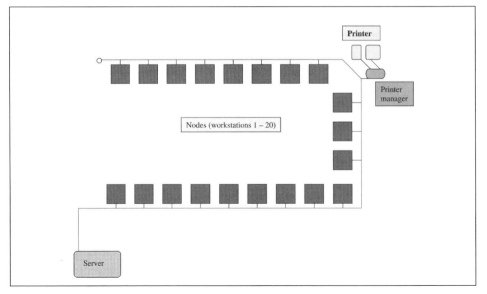

Figure 3.2   Network configuration at Grange Park School

Notes regarding the Grange Park setup
- The dark systems form the main part of the computer room and are standard PCs linked to the server somewhere else in the school. In this case, it is the room next door to one of the rooms.
- There are two printers in each computer room and the server is responsible for allocating one of the printers to a workstation as soon as printing facilities are requested. The printer manager is a piece of hardware that links to both printers. In this setup, the server has a piece of software which keeps track of the printing done by individuals and this is used for monitoring purposes: it is important that students do not abuse their printing privileges by wasting paper and ink.
- The server cannot be used as a computer in its own right: it is the managing agent for the workstations in each room.

Names and passwords ensure that only registered users have access to the equipment and there can be other security procedures set up as well. For example, the network can be set up so that a student doesn't have access to the right button on the mouse. If active, this button can create havoc as illustrated by the resources available to the user in Figure 3.3: in this case, by right clicking over the Microsoft Office icon, it is possible to delete the folder that contains the Microsoft software.

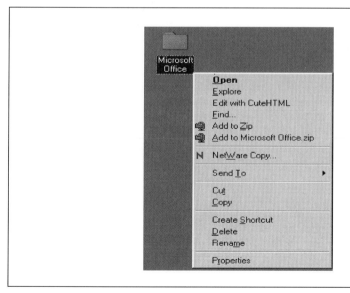

Figure 3.3   All the things you can do if you have access to the right-hand button on a PC mouse

Hardware resourcing: Meadowhall School

Meadowhall School has a central server in the IT office. Applications software such as Microsoft Office is loaded on the server, while department-specific software is loaded onto individual hard drives in an appropriate computer room to reduce traffic on the network. There are five computer rooms all linked to the network. The library has stand-alone computers.

Each student has a username and password to enable him or her to access the network. Teachers also have individual passwords. Students can access only folders allocated to them by the network manager. Each folder is available to a specific year group, which means for instance, Year 8 can access only particular software that has been allocated to them. They do not see other year group folders on their desktop once logged on.

The school is linked to the LEA intranet where a filter is set to prevent students from accessing unauthorised sites on the Internet. If the school needs further access outside the LEA provision, it has to approach the LEA for authorisation.

Unlike Grange Park, the school has a network manager (a non-teaching role) who has the responsibility of maintaining all the hardware and software in the school and is part of the management team.

Rationale

At Meadowhall School, there is an ICT manager who is responsible for the networking and this role is non-teaching. Gradually, schools are beginning to employ technical support but it has been a long time coming. Technical support and advice are essential for the smooth running of a hardware resource and there is no logic in having this role combined with a teaching commitment.

Most local authorities have an intranet system that gives schools access to the web in a stated context of security. Intranets like this limit access to approved sites only.

In schools where computers are not networked, there are many management issues which have to be dealt with. A major problem centres on the lack of centralisation of data with non-networked setups. If you want to continue working on a document, you will have to have it on a floppy disk or go to the computer last used, if it is saved on the hard disk.

All these issues and many more have to be considered when setting up and running an ICT resource and it is important that in a subject that is continually changing, hardware developments such as cost, processors and memory are regularly reviewed.

Issues related to purchasing hardware

When a school purchases computers and related hardware, the research involved in this is no different from the research an individual would undertake to buy a home computer: there will be a stated budget and a list of essential and desirable components. It is worthwhile producing this list in a generic format in the first instance and then breaking it down with specific, up-to-date costs. It is not the purpose of this section to give specific prices as they will certainly be out of date quickly. However, by stating generic issues, the solutions to these issues have a chance of being relevant as you read this.

The purchase of an individual computer or a computer suite should not be looked at as being a once-in-a-lifetime purchase: specifications change on a daily basis and if you are buying hardware in order to use a broad range of applications regularly then you will probably need to update it after three years. This equally applies to a school purchase where systems will get much more use by more students. The following is a list of items to consider prior to purchase and could equally be the questions you would ask yourself individually or as a potential buyer for a school suite.

A list of items to consider
1. Do I need a desktop computer or a laptop? What will it be used for?
2. How much main memory **random-access memory** **(RAM)** will I need to run the applications that I want?
3. How much hard disk space will enable me to store the required applications and give me room for growth?
4. Is the purchase part of a longer-term plan?
5. What size screen would I prefer?
6. What is my budget?
7. How will I backup my work?

Possible solutions to the above
1. For an individual purchase, if you are limited for space then a laptop is ideal; laptops are equally powerful and more convenient. School purchases should be considered further: as hardware resources grow, laptops may be the answer as a smaller-scale resource dispersible

throughout the school. The example from Grange Park School illustrates the use of laptops outside of the main resource, managed through Science. Further portable computer purchases are discussed later in this chapter.

2. For an individual purchase, it is always worth having as much RAM as possible. Whatever software you buy will soon be updated and this will include several new features. Invariably, new features improve the product and take up more memory. The more RAM you have, the faster everything will work. It is worth specifying extra RAM rather than upgrading it yourself. The same applies for school purchases except that it is important that the server has even more memory than the workstations as it will have more work to do. The price of RAM varies and is often in short supply.

3. For both individual and school purchases, you need to ensure that there is enough hard disk space to store the software you want to install, but that isn't the end of it. Growth needs to be considered as does the type of files that will be stored. For example, images can take up much space if stored in certain generic formats such as **bit mapped**. Such files have a .bmp extension. Having said this, most computers now have adequate size hard disks for the expected life of the system. For a school purchase, there are further networking issues (if a network is required). The server needs to have a larger hard disk than the workstations because of the extra networking software needed. Also, it depends on the network configuration of software: if all of the application software is installed and used from the server, then it needs to be larger than if the application software is installed and used locally at a workstation.

4. As mentioned before, any computer purchase, individually or for a school, should not be seen as a final solution to the problem: computers have a limited life so it is important to buy the best available at the time. School purchases will need expert advice regarding the buying of a server and such advice is readily available from manufacturers and dealers.

5. Screen size is important and the choice is not as straightforward as it used to be. Ideally the screen size should be no smaller than 15 inches, 17 inches being ideal. There is also the option of newer flat screens, which cost considerably more than the others.

6. Budget usually dictates all of the above but there are two issues, above all, which will be decided by the finance available: whether to go for a Pentium processor or one of the others such as AMD or Celeron and whether to buy a known make such as Hewlett Packard or Compaq or

a not-so-well-known make. Often the known make can cost twice as much.

7. Individual backup of data can be done in several ways: copying documents onto a rewritable CD is an easy option, whereas for school backup security, there needs to be a regular specified structure in place and on a network this is usually done with a backup tape device, timed to backup at stated intervals, for example, once each day. Such a device is expensive but needs to be costed into a school purchase because of the potential disaster looming without it.

Activity 3.1
Are there hardware purchasing issues missed out of the above? Discuss the methods your school uses to purchase hardware with the ICT coordinator.

Issues related to purchasing software

Implicit in the discussion above is that software will also need to be purchased and there are many issues associated with software purchasing for both the school and individuals. The first issue relates to the hardware setup being through either a network or stand alone systems. If the school has a network, then software purchasing will be done through a licence. For example, if you want Microsoft Office 2000 on a 20-system network then you will buy a licence to install it on 20 systems: you will not receive 20 individual CDs but one with a certificate giving the right to install on 20 systems. Also, the cost will not be 20 times an individual purchase; it will be less. Educational prices are also much less than purchasing as an individual in a typical discount outlet.

I have mentioned Microsoft Office because it is a popular product across all PCs, in business, commerce and education, and most teachers have access to it either at home or in school. It is important that there is a consistency of software purchasing in schools so that compatibility between home and school can be achieved. Have you ever been in a position where a file you have produced at home will not load onto a system at school? Most applications are now backwardly compatible; for example, a file saved on Word 2000 will automatically load onto Word 97, but compatibility issues do need looking at during purchase. Files saved in Publisher 2000 will not backwardly load into Publisher 98, for example, but there are usually ways to ensure that work saved can go between different versions of software.

A school network will have different types of software on it in order to serve different purposes: Microsoft Office or an equivalent will be there as a support for all curriculum subjects whereas a version of Logo may be there to support Maths at Key Stage 3. Other subjects may have software dedicated for use within that subject.

Portable computers

In this chapter, we have discussed many issues related to hardware and software organisation and purchasing in the secondary school. These discussions have focused on the centralised resourcing of hardware more than the dispersment of hardware at different locations in the school. The use of portable computers should not be ignored when thinking about purchases outside a central resource and this final section will look at what types of portable computers are available. I have inevitably mentioned some specific brand names in this discussion but as you will see, there is still a generic side to the discussion that shows to be a timeless feature of portables. The first generic issue is that of *size*.

Portable computers come in a range of sizes and as a result can be classified as either *palmtop* or *laptop*. There are other names given, such as *pocketbook* (for palmtop) and *notebook* (for laptop), and the distinction lies in the portability and facilities contained within them. The focus here is the purchasing of either types for use across specific curriculum subjects.

The palmtop

Over the years, Psion has dominated this section of the market and it still produces a range of systems varying in price and facilities. The original hardware, although having a Windows type working environment, had no mouse and input was solely through the keyboard. The Psion 3c exemplifies this and is illustrated in Figure 3.4.

The Psion 3c gradually came down in price from £399 to approximately £150 and has found its way into many schools. Palmtop purchases are generally seen as an additional resource to the main setup. The facilities offered by this system are substantial in that they contain a word processor, spreadsheet and database which are all compatible with standard desktop software. In addition, the Psion 3c can be linked to standard PC hardware.

Figure 3.4   Psion 3c palmtop

Using palmtops: St James School

At St James School, the ICT coordinator had the use of ten Psion 3c palmtops over a one-year period through a research project set up through a local university. She maintained a log of usage. The school has a centralised resource and the ICT coordinator is responsible for taking classes into the resource as well as having a staff development role. She was keen to involve the staff in using the palmtops for their own professional development. What follows are some extracts from her log of the experience.

I personally have found the Psion 3c to be invaluable and one has taken up residence in my bag.... I have compiled parts of the school ICT policy in a Word document. This was an ongoing operation which occurred at any convenient time and place.... Using the Spreadsheet, I was able to compile data on all members of staff who had undergone ICT INSET [in-service training]. This told me whether they had tuition on our new PCs, laptops and/or palmtops.... When I teach ICT, I use a palmtop to record the activity and achievements of the children.

My recording is done as the children are working at the computer. At the end of the session I add my recommendations, so that the class teacher has an idea of what ICT activities to concentrate on until my next session with that class. I save this in Word as a Rich Text File, transfer it to a school PC, and print off two copies. I give one copy to the class teacher and one goes in my file.... I have used palmtops with small groups of children as an introduction to word processing.... Generally I have groups of five or six children, each with a palmtop.

Our ICT technician used a palmtop to collect and collate the serial numbers of the new school PCs. This information was then transferred to the PC and printed out for the school records.

Because the take-up for the palmtops is increasing we are making a timetable so that staff can sign up for the palmtops to be used during a specified session within their class, which makes planning a lot easier for the class teacher. At the end of the session the work is usually saved and transferred to a PC and then printed out. The printouts are then returned to the class teacher as evidence of the children's achievements.

The ICT coordinator looks upon the palmtops as a resource for staff development and although this is in its infancy, there are clear signs of acceptance of this new resource. Staff are able to take them home as well and this has also been a useful facility. Enabling staff to take hardware off site has also had good results in the DfEE-funded Laptops Project (details available from the BECTA website at www.becta.org.uk) where an important staff development initiative was to allow teachers to take the laptops home, to work in their own environment.

Alongside the Psion 3c came the Psion 5 and Revo and these systems have touch screen facilities through a pen and a true Windows environment. Figure 3.5 illustrates the Revo, which has 16 mb of main memory.

Figure 3.5   Psion Revo

The software environment on the Revo is closer to the true Windows-type software than the Psion 3c and the transfer of documents is much easier.

Activity 3.2
When would a portable resource such as a palmtop be useful in your curriculum subject? List a range of exercises in which a portable would score over a desktop.

The laptop

The laptop computer is equally as powerful as the desktop in all ways. A laptop will cost more than the equivalent desktop but, as with the palmtop, has portability on its side. Toshiba are renowned for their laptops but many other manufacturers produced competitively priced alternatives. The specifications for laptops are the same as for desktops but there are other issues to consider before purchasing. For example, although it is easy to connect a mouse to all laptops, they also have the equivalent through either a track pad or a button located between keys in the keyboard. Many teachers have said that the button is difficult to use whereas the track pad can be mastered more quickly. As with the palmtop, the laptop should be considered for purchase for use where both portability and space are issues. Some schools are already purchasing laptops for use with small groups of students to good effect. It is worth revisiting the report of the Laptops Project through BECTA (www.becta.org.uk) to see how they can be useful for your own professional development.

Summary

In this chapter, I have discussed the broad range of roles and responsibilities of the ICT coordinator. The role usually extends to having responsibility for ICT as a subject as well as playing a major part in the purchasing of hardware and software. The coordinator has a difficult job keeping up to date with the subject and the best scenario is where there is an ICT coordinator, a subject specialist responsible for the ICT subject and technical support to solve the many problems that can and do occur with networked and non-networked computers. The examples discussed in this chapter suggest that these are achievable but that support needs to be given from senior management.

Solutions to activities

Activity 3.1

There are several possibilities here and they could relate to departmental requirements such as the need for a scanner in Art. All schools have their own in-house requirements but most use a PC-based resource along with a Microsoft Office base of software. It is useful to discuss hardware purchasing with a school local to yours, as often there are deals to be done. The LEA usually has recommendations for schools and these can also be taken into consideration.

Activity 3.2

A geography field trip immediately comes to mind here: collecting data at source and transferring to a desktop for further analysis.

Most palmtops can be used for data logging: they can be left to record data over a period of time, for example, light or temperature, and again, these data can be transferred to a desktop application such as Excel for further analysis.

All kinds of palmtops are useful when conducting research: the portable nature and good battery life enables them to be used in libraries and in locations not conducive for using other hardware.

Reference

NCET (1998) *IT Coordination in Secondary Schools*, Information Sheet. London: NCET.

CHAPTER 4

ICT in primary schools

The objectives of this chapter are as follows:

- To investigate the use of ICT in primary schools
- To illustrate good practice through a mini case study
- To provide issues for consideration for the primary–secondary transfer stage.

The primary–secondary transfer: the need for discussion

Before we discuss the issues of delivering ICT in the secondary school, it is important to be aware of the background that students have from their primary schools. It is only with this understanding and knowledge that adequate planning can take place for the primary–secondary transfer. The assessments that students take with them to the secondary school should ensure that there is continuity and it is unfortunate that there are many OFSTED references to Year 7 students underachieving in ICT. However, there are now signs of continuity, particularly where the secondary ICT coordinator visits feeder primary schools during the Summer term of transfer.

The national numeracy and literacy strategies have, in some cases, encouraged primary and secondary teachers to establish a link. This is particularly useful since at Key Stage 3, secondary teachers have to plan and deliver numeracy in the same format as primary teachers – in the three-part lesson format. Secondary Maths teachers are undergoing training to achieve this and in many cases, it is something quite new. Through these two strategies, along with a developing ICT transfer policy, there are signs that Key Stage 3 will build on the primary experiences of students.

The primary ICT problem: breadth and depth

Primary schools have much more of a tradition for integrating ICT across the curriculum; the primary curriculum involves one teacher teaching a range of subjects, sometimes with the help of others, sometimes not. The primary teacher will usually have a subject specialism but this may have been developed without the use of ICT, particularly if the teacher has been qualified for more than five years. However, through the different training routes now available for primary teachers, most NQTs of primary have used ICT within a range of subjects in the same way that secondary trainee teachers have, through the ICT audit discussed in Chapter 2. Their task is made more difficult though, through the 'jack of all trades' approach that is necessary for a primary teacher to deliver all of the National Curriculum.

The implication for having a breadth of subject knowledge spanning all the curriculum subjects is that ICT will play an appropriate part in these subjects; the primary teachers' view of ICT needs to be holistic. Of course, this is nothing new; in Chapter 1, I discussed the original software supplied to primary schools in the guise of the Microprimer package and although the software was rather primitive, it was easy to see that most curriculum subjects were represented. Software is now much better and where ICT is being used effectively, it is still supporting a range of subjects.

Hardware organisation in the primary school

Over the years, primary schools have acquired a range of hardware and until recently, this has been by purchasing Acorn hardware. The Acorn Archimedes prevailed during the 1990s but now the tendency is for primary schools to purchase PC hardware. This makes much sense since it is the platform that is usually available in the secondary school and where children have computers at home, they are also usually PCs.

In terms of organisation, the traditional primary model has been a distributed one with one or more computers in the classroom. This is logical since the computer has always been seen as a support tool for the other curriculum subjects and by having ICT equipment on hand, there theoretically seems to be a better chance to use it as and when it is required. This has been the thinking behind many school setups in the past but there are an increasing number of schools who are looking towards the ICT lab, a dedicated resource where whole classes can go during a timetabled slot.

Activity 4.1
- What advantages are there in organising hardware in an ICT lab?
- Can you see any disadvantages?

By thinking about Activity 4.1, you will have no doubt discussed the practicalities of delivering the primary curriculum through an organisational structure similar to that found in the secondary school, as a means of ensuring that children get as much ICT usage as possible. The following case study exemplifies one school's approach to the delivery of ICT through the construction of an ICT lab. This case study also provides an all-round approach which gives the secondary school a sound base to develop.

An ICT lab: St John's C of E Primary School
At St John's, the head teacher has adopted an approach which provides a PC network in a dedicated room (Figure 4.1). The network has 15 workstations and in addition to this there are 2 PCs in each classroom, as well as additional PCs in the SEN room and library. Every workstation that is attached to the network has unlimited Internet access through an open **asymmetric digital subscriber line (ADSL)** which is protected by the filtering software Net Nanny to limit undesirable access.

A class set of 30 AlphaSmart portable word processors allow additional support of ICT anywhere with direct downloading to any desktop computer.

Also available for use are several digital cameras, data logging equipment, a Roamer, inkjet printers and several scanners in both the computer lab and classrooms.

Figure 4.1   St John's ICT lab, a network of PCs timetabled throughout the week

The ICT coordinator and policy
Most primary schools have an ICT Policy and this is usually developed by the ICT coordinator. The coordinator will usually be a member of staff who has an incentive responsibility allowance for the work and may (or may not) have an ICT qualification. In the case of St John's, the ICT coordinator has been teaching for three years and opted to undertake a four-year teacher training degree with ICT (named Computer Education at the time) as a main subject. The training course focused on issues of ICT delivery and management and this proved to give him a useful starting point.

Aims for using ICT in school
Our aims for the use of ICT in school are that all children will be given the opportunity to:

- apply ICT to all appropriate applications with confidence and a sense of achievement
- develop practical skills in the use of ICT and the ability to apply these skills to the solving of relevant and worthwhile problems
- understand the capabilities and limitations of ICT and consequences of its use.

Aims for using ICT in the classroom
ICT can be taught as a discrete subject but also as a tool to be used as appropriate throughout the curriculum to support children's learning. In order to ensure that valuable areas of experience are covered:

- ICT use is linked to other subjects (where appropriate)
- computer use is managed to ensure that all pupils are given equal access opportunities – following the equal opportunities policy
- ICT use is not to be withdrawn as a punishment or given as a reward.

The grouping of children will depend on the task being undertaken. Pupils with special educational needs have the same entitlement as all other pupils and are offered the same curriculum. In addition, ICT can be used to target those children with specific learning difficulties and children with high ability.

Homework is not used to support specific activities, as access to home computers is variable. Each class will be timetabled the portable AlphaSmarts to carry out at least one piece of word-processed work at home. In addition to this, teachers will allow computer-generated homework when it is appropriate to the set task.

The emphasis in our teaching with ICT is on the use of computers as tools to support learning. Excellence in ICT is celebrated in demonstrations and display including:

- demonstrations at parent–teacher consultations and open days.
- display around the school of text, pictures, graphs and charts that have been produced by pupils using ICT.

The role of the ICT coordinator
The role of the ICT co-ordinator is to:

- take the lead in policy development and the integration of ICT into schemes of work designed to ensure progression and continuity throughout the school

- support colleagues in their efforts to include ICT in their development of detailed work plans, in their implementation of those schemes of work and in assessment and record keeping activities
- monitor progress in ICT and inform the headteacher on action needed
- take responsibility for the purchase and organisation of central resources for ICT
- provide technical support to colleagues in their use of ICT in the classroom
- pass on information to colleagues as appropriate.

Assessment, recording and reporting to ensure continuity
All teachers will submit half-termly plans reflecting the scheme of work as well as updating the annual overview for ICT, copies of which will be in each class's planning file as well as the ICT coordinator's file.

Feedback to pupils about their progress is usually given while a task is being carried out through discussion between child and teacher.

Formative assessment is used to guide the progress of individual pupils in their use of ICT. It involves identifying each child's progress, determining what each child has learned and what therefore should be the next stage of their learning. Each unit of work includes an 'Integrated Task'. This should be used as a formal assessment opportunity of a child's learning through that unit. Electronic copies of all work undertaken are kept on the main server in each pupil's individual file.

When recording the achievement of a child, class teachers will record the levels of attainment based upon the National Curriculum at the end of each term (in KS2) and in accordance with the school's ongoing assessment policy. Reporting to parents will focus on the child's ability to use a computer with confidence and competence across a variety of applications. This will be carried out through termly interviews and the end of year written report.

Table 4.1   Extract from St John's ICT Policy

Table 4.1. comprises an extract from the ICT Policy. In many ways, the structure of ICT coordination in the primary school is no different from that in the secondary school, particularly where the secondary coordinator is not the head of department. Secondary schools should be thinking along the lines of a discrete coordinator who can offer support within the curriculum subjects but is not responsible for post Key Stage 3 subject specific ICT teaching; this can be left to the specialist. The primary teacher has a harder job according to the ICT Policy illustrated, through the clear statements regarding assessment recording and reporting. It is a requirement that ICT is used by all teachers in the school. All classes have a timetabled slot in the ICT lab and have to give termly forecasts of their work. These forecasts are reported to parents and are published on the web. Some extracts of these forecasts for the Summer term are as follows:

- **Reception:** The computer is ever popular and the children are using software to work on basic Maths and English skills as well as improving their keyboard skills. During this term it is hoped they will have the opportunity to use the ICT lab where they will be able to enjoy more challenging and exciting activities.
- **Year 3:** We will have weekly lessons in the ICT lab. This half-term we will be continuing learning about email and using the Internet to find information about specific subjects. Next half-term we will be going over what we have learnt about databases: what they are and how to create and manipulate our own. We will be using a program called Primary Toolkit and will also be going on the Internet. Please be assured that all work on the Internet is closely supervised by myself and will happen within a tight framework of known sites; there will be no exploration at this early stage.
- **Year 5:** Classroom ICT will focus on research by using the web and CD-ROMs to access information to complement our literacy, numeracy, humanities and independent projects. Lab-based work for the beginning of term will include the use of control technology and programming the Roamer through Logo.
- **Year 6:** The class will have the opportunity to work within Hyperstudio, a multimedia package, which will allow them to set up an on-screen project of work relating to their study of Cornwall. The class will be able to add buttons and sounds to pages, fade pictures in and out and may possibly create their own animations to add to their study. They will also have access to the AlphaSmarts for the majority of this term to allow them to carry out research at home and transfer their work into Hyperstudio.

You can see that there are some complex activities taking place here, for example, the use of authoring software in the form of Hyperstudio. This could be developed in Year 7 if the secondary school is aware of it taking place in Year 6. There would be problems in that not all primary feeder schools use Hyperstudio but knowing that Year 6 students can develop applications with it suggests that it can be done. Not many Year 7 students get the opportunity to use authoring software.

The web has been mentioned across several year groups and this is an ever increasing area for development in primary schools. St John's has produced its own web pages which include much documentation for parents as well as examples of student's work.

Figure 4.2 illustrates the home page at www.StJohnsWhetstone.co.uk and Figure 4.3 is an example of a poem from a Year 5 student.

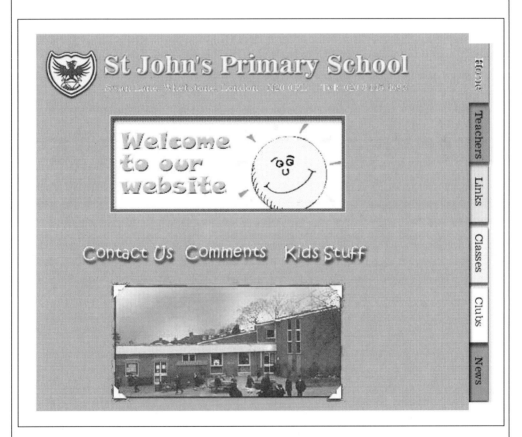

Figure 4.2   St John's School home page

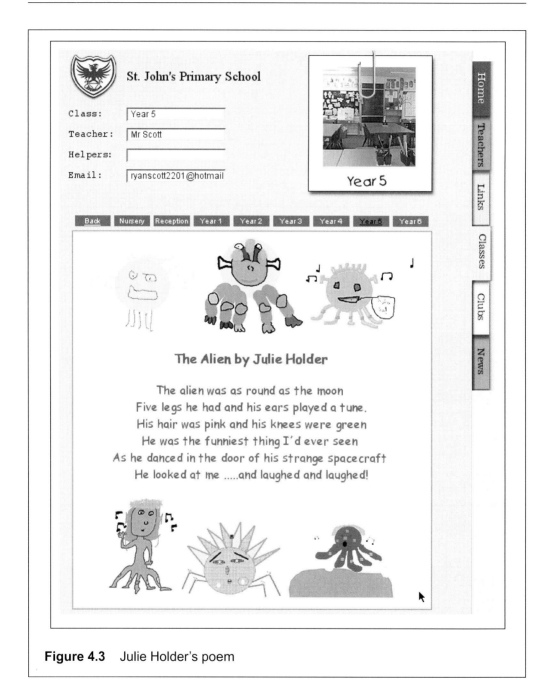

Figure 4.3 Julie Holder's poem

Summary

Secondary schools should make reference to the ICT work achieved during the primary years, particularly at Key Stage 2. A recent OFSTED (2001) annual report suggests that primary ICT trends are improving:

Achievement in IT in Key Stage 1 has risen in many schools. For example, pupils in Year 2 increasingly handle equipment and software independently. They understand a screen display of icons and manipulate the keyboard and mouse effectively to exercise options and to drag images ... A strength of pupils' work is in the communications aspects of IT, especially if pupils have access to computers at home. Although many pupils at the end of Y2 are still slow at entering text, they are increasingly effective in searching for, and downloading, material from on-line sources. Use of the Internet motivates pupils significantly, particularly where they find material of real interest.

And at Key Stage 2:

There has been a sustained improvement in pupils' manipulation of graphics and of visual media in Key Stage 2, and in their ability to combine graphics, text and sound for a presentation. This reflects higher attainment in the sense that pupils do not only use striking IT effects and animations in their work, but also consider their suitability for readers or users... Increasingly, pupils are gaining from the application of IT to other subjects, especially in Key Stage 2 when applying their data handling and presentation skills. For example, application in science, geography or mathematics enables pupils to practise and improve their skills in building and using a database.

Students are entering secondary schools with a broad range of experiences and we should be using these experiences as a foundation for the planning of the Key Stage 3 ICT curriculum, whether it is taught as a discrete subject or integrated through other subjects. The case study discussed shows a whole-school approach with assessment opportunities carefully timed during the year.

Solution to Activity 4.1

The main advantage in having an ICT lab in a primary school is one of centralisation. Classes will need to be timetabled into the lab and so it can be seen that there are specific times when classes will use ICT. Of course, a timetabled slot makes the process and use rather mechanistic and requires planning by individual class teachers; there needs to be work prepared for use during the slot. For example, if a group are working on word processing a piece of work, a strategy may be to print out the work at the end of an ICT session and redraft it on the printout for the next time.

The above discussion has alluded to the disadvantage of a lack of spontaneity when using ICT. Many teachers have suggested that this is the case although it is difficult to see how the alternative, i.e. having hardware in the class, has ever facilitated reasonable ICT access because there has simply never been adequate hardware resourcing to have enough computers in each class.

Reference

OFSTED (2001) OFSTED Subject Report, 1999–2000, Information Technology, available on the web at
http://www.OFSTED.gov.uk/public/docs01/subjects/subjects99–00.htm

PART 3

ICT across the 11–18 age range

CHAPTER 5

ICT at Key Stage 3

The objectives of this chapter are as follows:

- To investigate models of ICT delivery at Key Stage 3
- To place these models in a historical context
- To provide examples of the practical applications of ICT within two specific curriculum areas
- To identify the common misconceptions associated with ICT development.

There used to be considerable debate about the distinction between ICT and IT which seems rather irrelevant now as all examinable courses are being renamed from IT to ICT. One teacher said to me that the C (for communication) has crept into IT as the subject has broadened; I like this idea and like to think that it is entirely appropriate to refer to an examinable course such as A level ICT in the same way as using ICT to refer to a component within English, such as the use of a word processor to draft and redraft text.

Such debates have not taken place across Europe; ICT has simply replaced IT following the huge technological developments of the 1990s. The current UK National Curriculum reflects the change to ICT. Also, schools employ ICT specialists now and although there is no national job description for an ICT specialist, newly qualified teachers from IT PGCE courses will be the teachers applying for such positions.

ICT is taught in many ways and it is interesting to look at the implications for the different curriculum organisations currently adopted across the UK.

Models of ICT delivery at Key Stage 3

Even though there is no standard method for delivering ICT, it is possible to classify the model of delivery in one of two ways: the discrete ICT delivery model and the integrated ICT delivery model. Schools that have an integrated approach may also deliver some elements of ICT discretely (this is discussed later in the chapter). Assessment forms a vital part of any ICT structure and some important elements related to the examples are discussed in Chapter 6.

Discrete ICT delivery model

Discrete ICT operates within a school when students have dedicated ICT lessons. These lessons can be called ICT, IT, Information Systems or other variations. They often take the form of a one-hour block in Years 7 and 8 (and possibly 9) and are generally taught by the ICT specialist. The focus of this lesson is usually ICT and does not always relate to other curriculum subjects. There are a range of issues associated with ICT delivery in this way. The implications for staffing are considerable and we are now seeing a shift away from the ICT coordinator delivering everything to the inclusion of staff from other curriculum areas.

  The following two case studies illustrate different approaches to discrete ICT delivery.

Discrete ICT model 1: Epping St John School
Epping operates the discrete ICT model; all students have a weekly 45-minute lesson within the following structure:
Year 7 All students are introduced to a standard range of software including word processing (Word), spreadsheets (Excel) and an introduction to **desk top publishing (DTP** through Publisher). The subject focus is ICT and it is delivered by the ICT coordinator along with another member of staff, who is part-time. Where possible, the coordinator tries to ensure that the content of the lessons relates to another curriculum area, but the main focus of the lessons is to become familiar with the software. An initial audit of ICT skills takes place during the first term in order for lesson planning to reflect differentiation of abilities and skills gained in the primary school. The coordinator visits primary schools during the Summer term and is keen to ensure that the transition from primary to secondary is as smooth as possible.

Year 8   Students continue to build on the skills developed in Year 7. They produce further material using Publisher and are introduced to Databases (Access). Again, the focus is clearly on the software and a database is set up and developed with regard to a fictitious firm. Students have to conduct a significant amount of research during the year and the implications for using ICT to develop and present this work are prominent.

Year 9   The ICT coordinator suggests that students should have become familiar with the software over the previous two years; the coordinator now takes on more of an ICT management role. Students are expected to work on another project based within the local community. There is a distinct move away from the software skills focus, in that students have to use familiar software to design a business as well as other individual tasks which address the criteria not met through the project. The project involves questionnaire design and analysis, the production of advertising material, the sending out of business letters and the analysis of business predictions. For more able students, the role of ICT in the process is discussed. This leads on to GCSE ICT coursework as all students take the short course in Year 11.

Students keep a file of work over the three years and this is the main contributor to the level awarded at the end of Year 9. Also, there are built-in assessment points and students are given regular written feedback on their progress.

Discrete ICT model 2: Davenant Foundation School
At the Davenant Foundation School, there is a similar approach in place but they are now making use of the **Qualifications and Curriculum Authority (QCA)** schemes of work for Key Stage 3 ICT. These documents break down ICT into manageable units and the school has developed assessment criteria for each unit. This helps the process of levelling at the end of the key stage.

At the end of each unit of work, students are assessed against National Curriculum levels, which are recorded on a spreadsheet in the shared staff area on the network. This informs the end of the key stage levelling exercise and ensures that a range of levels, attributed in a continuous, formative manner, contribute to the summative level in Year 9.

Students in Year 7 receive homework, which usually takes the form of any research and development element of the current unit. Students are not expected to use a computer for homework. Davenant sees the importance of setting ICT homework and always ensures that it links closely to the practical element of a project. A good example of this is the research and development required before using software to produce a questionnaire. Homework need not be focused on using software.

Timing of units

Table 5.1 illustrates when the QCA units are delivered during Years 7 and 8.

Year	Unit no.	Unit title	Teaching time (1-hour lessons)
7	1	Using ICT	4
7	2	Information and presentation	5
7	3	Processing text and images	7
7	4	Models: rules and investigations	5
7	5	Data: designing structure, capturing and presenting data	6
7	6	Control: input, process and output	5
7	7	Measuring physical data	4
8	8	Public information systems	7
8	9	Publishing on the web	7
8	10	Information: reliability, validity and bias	7
8	11	Data: use and misuse	3
8	12	Systems: integrating applications to find solutions	12

Figure 5.1   ICT Key Stage 3 schemes of work: unit titles and teaching times

An example: Unit 3 Processing Text and Images

The QCA scheme of work for this unit suggests that students work together in the production of a newspaper. This unit is illustrated in Table 5.2.

About the unit

In this unit pupils work in small groups to prepare a printed newspaper. They gather, process and output information in text and image form and explore a variety of image-capture and image-manipulation methods to create suitable image data. They learn to develop strategies of group working, including data sharing across networks. There are opportunities for links with English when pupils develop the text for the newspaper. Links could also be made to other subjects when choosing the topics for the articles, e.g. the weather, sport. The newspaper could be produced in another language, providing opportunities to collaborate with the modern foreign languages department. Note: in some areas the local press are happy to assist or contribute to such activities. It may also be possible to integrate this task within a single 'activity week'. This unit is expected to take approximately seven hours.

Where the unit fits in

This unit builds on the Key Stage 2 scheme of work, in particular Unit 3A' Combining text and graphics', Unit 4A 'Writing for different audiences', Unit 4B 'Developing images using repeating patterns', Unit 4D 'Collecting and presenting information: questionnaires and pie charts', Unit 5B 'Analysing data and asking questions: using complex searches' and Unit 5C 'Evaluating information, checking accuracy and questioning plausibility'.

Pupils may already have worked in small groups in ICT, and this unit will build on that practice. The unit also acts as an introduction to networking ICT resources.

Expectations

At the end of this unit most pupils will: work collectively to organise, refine and present a newspaper using a template designed through analysis of audience needs; identify image requirements, acquire and process images by the most appropriate method; share information freely among the group; apply their template and system to the production of further printed output.

Some pupils will not have made so much progress and will: work within a group and help in organising, refining and presenting a newspaper using a template; scan suitable images from identified sources; share information.

Some pupils will have progressed further and will: develop a process of newspaper production that divides tasks into clearly defined subtasks with clarity in the analysis and design of the solution (extra work may involve advanced processes, e.g. simulating pre-press production, creating separation film); manage and time subtasks; develop a range of appropriate template styles for a variety of uses.

Prior learning
It is helpful if pupils have:
- prior experience of using word-processing and desktop-publishing software
- used a 'painting' graphics package to produce their own pictures.

Extension and enrichment
Pupils could prepare content for their production using libraries and other resources. This unit could also form part of their preparation for a newspaper day. Content for the newspaper could be prepared in other subjects.

Table 5.2   Unit 3 Processing Text and Images (Source: QCA website at www.standards.dfes.gov.uk/schemes)

Davenant has stuck to the timings of each unit (seven hours in this case) and a problem with encouraging students to collaborate on the production of a newspaper is that it is difficult to assess individual progress as the work is taking place. Each group is carefully monitored and all members have to justify the individual work they have done, through illustration and discussion.

Students are given the criteria for the assignment and know what they need to do to achieve a certain level. These are discussed in Chapter 6.

It is interesting to place the discrete ICT delivery model in the context of the use of ICT within other subject areas. ICT was originally introduced as a tool at Key Stage 3 and through the development of the QCA schemes of work, it would seem that schools are being encouraged to implement a discrete delivery approach. This is only one interpretation of the QCA's work and there is no doubt that the skills that should be covered at Key Stage 3 are well catered for through the schemes. Many ICT teachers suggest that the only way to assess accurately ICT capability is through discrete ICT delivery; if there is good use of ICT across other curriculum subjects then this is a bonus.

Integrated ICT delivery model

The DfEE (1998) suggests that there is much to be made of the integrated approach and that integration within the subjects and collaboration between the subjects should be the way forward:

> many English teachers have used computers for creating electronic newspapers, which pupils produce with desktop publishing software. Good English work is sometimes produced, and the pressure of working to a tight production timetable throws into sharp relief the advantages of text and image handling by computer. Often, however, expectations of layout and visual attractiveness of such class publications are not high. Opportunities are rarely taken for involving teachers from art and design departments in jointly supervising and assessing such work. The application of IT to designing and making a product, such as a newspaper, offers opportunities for teachers with different subject backgrounds to be seen to work together in order to raise expectations and standards overall.
>
> (DfEE 1998: 24)

The above approach of integration within the subjects and between teachers of other subjects I will refer to as **multiple integration**: the staffing and management implications for achieving this suggest that it is not a regular structure in schools (indeed, as highlighted by the quoted report), but it is nevertheless a model to aim for. A possible compromise is to adopt a 'hybrid' model, as discussed by Crawford (1997). This model involves integrated use within subjects, topped up by discrete use in a timetable ICT slot. With the development of the QCA material, this may be the best approach to take but it is always important to build on what students have come with from both the primary school and the home.

Most schools use the **single integration** approach where the focus is within other curriculum subjects, as in the multiple approach, but where the non-ICT subject specialist uses ICT to deliver elements of the specialism and there is little, if any, input from the ICT specialist or other subject teachers.

Multiple integration model
One ICT coordinator discussed her approach to the multiple integration model as follows:

> At Key Stage 3, we feel that students should have the use of ICT within a specific curriculum subject. For example, all Year 8 students are introduced to PowerPoint at a time when they are developing a presentation in English – the English teacher provides the context for the lesson (a presentation about an author) although initially, she wasn't familiar with PowerPoint. We realise this will put a burden on the English teacher and so we have invested in double staffing this lesson: I am responsible for the ICT part of the lesson.

This structure has obvious advantages for students in that they can immediately see the context of ICT: PowerPoint is a content-free piece of software which has applications across all subjects. This particular school has spent one year double staffing Key Stage 3 ICT across the core National Curriculum subjects. It has been expensive but worthwhile. The English teacher taking this lesson alongside the ICT coordinator had little confidence at the start of the initiative but she gradually became familiar enough to use it on her own the following term. She commented as follows:

> I must admit that the thought of working alongside another member of staff was daunting because of my lack of expertise in ICT. My role was initially the role of a helper but it wasn't long before I was involved in discussing PowerPoint designs with the class. I knew what I wanted them to achieve so it wasn't as if I was doing it from scratch. Next time around, I will take the lesson myself having attended further ICT sessions after school and discussed the use of presentation software with other colleagues.

The context of ICT organisation

These two approaches to ICT delivery have a historical context outside of ICT; if we view the development of ICT in schools as an innovation, then the theories and models of Schon (1971) are particularly relevant. The Schon Center-Periphery Model helps us understand how innovations are disseminated. Why is ICT still an innovation? I feel that it is because in this context, the innovation has been gradually introduced over several years, is constantly changing and has a statutory delivery element to it.

Schon suggests that:

This model rests on 3 basic elements: the innovation to be diffused exists, fully realised in its essentials, prior to its diffusion. Diffusion is the movement of an innovation from a center out to its ultimate users. Directed diffusion is a centrally managed process of dissemination, training and provision of resources and incentives. Advocates of center-periphery theory have tended to see diffusion as the human interaction in which one person communicates a new idea to another person. Thus, at its most elemental level of conceptualisation, the diffusion process consists of (1) a new idea, (2) individual A who knows about the innovation and (3) individual B who does not know about the innovation.

(Schon 1971: 81)

Now of course, as ICT developments continue, individual B gradually knows a little more about the innovation but the ICT coordinator is still in the controlling position in a discrete delivery model, as illustrated in Figure 5.1.

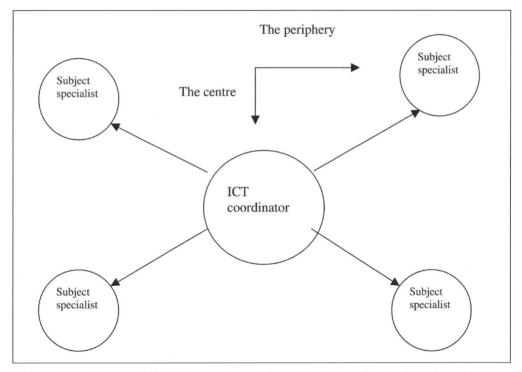

Figure 5.1   Discrete ICT delivery adapted from the Schon Center-Periphery Model

After a period of time, Schon suggests that each element on the periphery can become a centre itself, thus there is a proliferation of centres. Each centre has the knowledge and understanding associated with the original centre (well, almost!) and can act as a centre in its own right. In terms of ICT management, the 'new' centre can take over many of the functions of the 'original' centre (at least take over ICT delivery in the centre's own subject) and possibly disseminate to a new periphery, as illustrated in Figure 5.2.

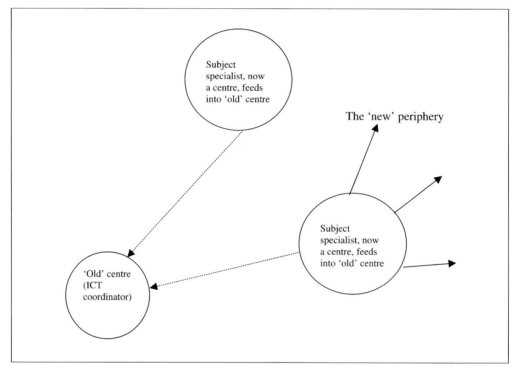

Figure 5.2   Integrated ICT delivery adapted from the Schon Center-Periphery Model

This kind of integrated approach can be identified in many schools: that is, the introduction of ICT through a coordinator, the staff gradually becoming ICT literate within their own subject and gradually the responsibility for subject-based ICT falling on the subject specialist, maybe with help and guidance from the overall ICT coordinator. Extrapolating from the Schon model, it could be argued that ultimately, there would be no need for an ICT coordinator, just devolved budgets to the departments. However, this is unlikely to happen because of the overall demand for a centralised hardware resource and with it, careful management by ICT specialists. It would not be practical to have departmental networks throughout, managed by departmental technicians. But there is no reason why a centralised resource cannot be managed centrally and used by subjects: in many schools, this is already happening.

ICT in Maths

This section and the next provide practical illustrations of the use of ICT within two curriculum subjects, Maths and Modern Foreign Languages. There are, of course, many other possible applications but those illustrated have been developed by the non-ICT specialist, that is, the teacher of another subject.

Logo

Logo is a structured computer programming language developed in the 1960s by Seymour Papert. For the rationale and philosophy behind Logo see Papert (1993). At Key Stage 3, students need to develop mathematical concepts in line with the Maths National Curriculum and there are many aspects that Logo can support. For example, within using and applying shape, space and measures, students should be able to:

- select problem-solving strategies and resources, including ICT, to use in geometric work
- interpret, discuss and synthesise geometrical information presented in a variety of forms
- distinguish between acute, obtuse, reflex and right angles; estimate the size of an angle in degrees. (DfEE 1999a: 36)

The approach to Logo in most secondary schools is quite different from the primary approach; the primary school often adopts an experimental approach to angle and turn whereas in the following context, the Key Stage 3 Maths curriculum provides the starting point. This is not to say that secondary students do not have similar misconceptions to primary students and of all subjects, it is worthwhile establishing a Logo audit in Year 7 because many feeder schools use Logo.

The structure of Logo

For Maths teachers to feel confident to deliver Logo at Key Stage 3, it is important that they have a grounding in the structure of the language and are able to troubleshoot when required.

Logo: Hazelwood School, Year 9

At Hazelwood, a Maths teacher has introduced Logo through working with the ICT coordinator during sessions after school; Logo takes the form of a module contained in Maths, although there is a distinct programming feel to it. It isn't until students feel confident in elements of the Logo language that the mathematical content is explored in any depth. Inherent in the approach is that by breaking down processes into manageable chunks, the student will gain a firm understanding of the processes involved in computer programming as well as further developing concepts of angle, shape and space.

Also, the number of students taking GCSE ICT has increased dramatically in recent years and this module forms the basis of a prior programming awareness module for the GCSE course.

MSW Logo is used because it is downloaded free from the web at www.softronix.com . Also, there are many examples of teaching material available for Logo on the site and it is well worth a look.

The programming concepts involved in this example can be broken down into the following five stages. Each stage has associated worksheets and they are designed for students to work on them autonomously. The worksheets include both maths and programming concepts and are linked to other work taking place in the 'standard' Maths lessons. The Logo module is delivered one hour each week for six weeks. All homework is paper based and students have to bring in solutions to programming tasks for subsequent lessons.

Stage 1: Immediate commands

Immediate commands are one-off instructions which enable you to draw shapes, starting at the centre of the screen. For example, the following commands draw a square. Note that forward and backward can be abbreviated to fd and bk and these represent movement in a straight line for the required number of units. Left and right abbreviate to lt and rt and are turns through the specified degrees.

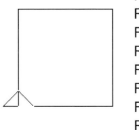

Forward 100
Right 90
Forward 100
Right 90
Forward 100
Right 90
Forward 100
Right 90

The mathematical concepts involved in the production of the square centre around the turning of an angle, in this case, the exterior angle of the square. One common misconception with students doing this is that they often think that they are turning through the interior angle of the square and not the exterior; of course, the angles are the same in this case but not in other shapes. If this were an equilateral triangle, the exterior angle would be 120 (not 60), as illustrated.

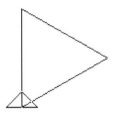

Forward 100
Right 120
Forward 100
Right 120
Forward 100
Right 120

It can be clearly seen that to produce these shapes, there needs to be an awareness of angles of turn.

Stage 2: Loops
The above example can be developed further in many ways. For example, from the programming perspective, the code typed in to produce the shape is inefficient; a loop could have been used to repeat the first two instructions as follows:

Repeat 3[Forward 100 Right 120]

The brackets are there simply to contain the instructions which are to be repeated.

From the mathematical perspective, using a loop to draw various regular shapes should result in the 'spotting' of the relationship between the exterior angle and the number of sides, i.e. the total number of degrees turned through (the sum of the exterior angles) is 360 and each angle of turn is 360 divided by the number of sides. The exterior angle of a pentagon is therefore 360/5 = 72 and the sequence of instructions to draw it is as follows:

Repeat 5[Forward 100 Right 72]

Stage 3: Including commands in a procedure

If you wanted to draw the shape above several more times, you would need to reuse the code given. However, you can give an instruction to remember the code in the form of a procedure, i.e. a sequence of instructions that relate to a specified name. It would seem sensible to call the above shape *pentagon*. The procedure would look as follows:

```
To Pentagon
      Repeat 5[Forward 100 Right 72]
End
```

Then, each time you type *pentagon*, the sequence of instructions is executed and a pentagon is drawn.

Stage 4: The use of variables

It is possible to produce a sequence of instructions to draw a polygon where the number of sides is stated *before* it is drawn through the use of a variable. The following procedure is a generic procedure to draw a polygon. The number of sides of the polygon is passed to the procedure in the command to draw it, and the relationship between the number of sides and the angle of turn is recognised by reusing the variable to calculate the degree required. The quotes and colon are part of the Logo syntax.

```
To "Polygon :sides
    Repeat :sides[Forward 100 Right 360/:sides]
End
```

By typing *Polygon 3* an equilateral triangle is drawn, *Polygon 4* a square. The following now seems quite achievable. It is for many Year 9 students!

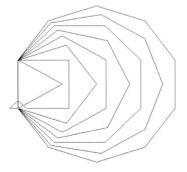

Polygon 3
Polygon 4
Polygon 5
Polygon 6
Polygon 7
Polygon 8
Polygon 9
Polygon 10

You can use more than one variable. For example, you could specify the length of the polygon as well as the number of sides:

```
To "Polygon :sides :length
    Repeat :sides[Forward :length Right 360/:sides]
End
```

Typing *Polygon 3 100* will draw an equilateral triangle of length 100.

Logo provides an excellent introduction to programming; the logical processes involved in programming should not be the reserve of Key Stage 4 and beyond; there is much educational worth to teaching programming as early as possible, particularly through Logo within a Maths context.

The use of spreadsheets: scroll bars in Excel

The following case study is an edited version of an article by Peter Mulkerrins (2000).

Excel: Penrice Community College

At Penrice College, Peter Mulkerrins has tailored the use of Excel with the powerful function of scroll bars and includes them into Excel worksheets. The work discussed is developed for Year 9.

It is worth remembering that it is quite possible to feel that you understand and can interact with spreadsheets well, and yet only really use 5 per cent of the inherent facilities available to you; the use of scroll bars is particularly relevant here as many experienced users of spreadsheets are not aware of the facilities available.

There are a range of set sequences that have to be worked through in the setting up of the scroll bar facilities and once this has been done, you can use it to create dynamic spreadsheets which will change as you move the scroll bar. The scroll bar provides an ideal way to control the variables on your sheet. They can then be used individually or you can have several on the same worksheet.

Peter Mulkerrins developed a set of sheets to explore the effects of reflections on coordinates. By changing the values in a range of scroll bars, he wanted the students to be able to quickly change the line of reflection and see the effects they would have on the image and its coordinates. To provide the quick change, he has used a scroll bar to change the equations of the mirror lines. The worksheets then display the coordinates of the image as the graph is produced.

This Year 9 class are working at levels 6 to 8+ and so were able students. Many of them will have used spreadsheets before but not within this context. Also, the activity has strength in that it clearly develops number pattern investigation at the same time as building on their capability to use and interpret spreadsheets using higher order thinking skills.

The aim was to investigate number patterns, find an algebraic connection and link these to the spatial properties. They were given the task of predicting the coordinates of the image given a x = ? line of reflection. A typical screen is illustrated in Figure 5.3 and the power of the slider bar can be seen as a dynamic tool in the discussions surrounding the exercise.

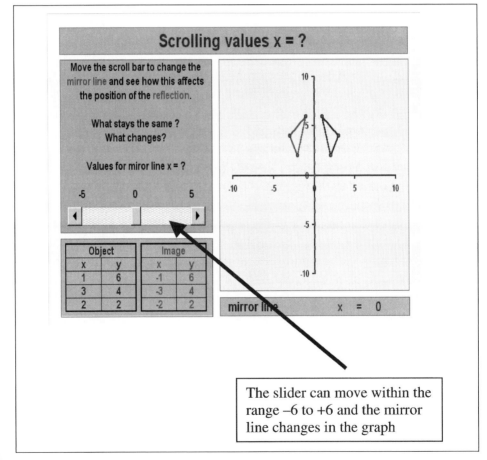

Figure 5.3   Using the slider

After a brief introduction to the spreadsheet, pupils worked in pairs for 50 minutes. The teacher circulated around the room listening and, through questioning, elicited explanations of what they had discovered and reinforced the importance of asking why?

All pupils noticed that the coordinate changed by two as the line of reflection changed by one and most discovered the connection

$$(x, y) \ddagger (2r - x, y)$$

where r is the value for the mirror line $x = r$. This prompted further discussions and connections and several in the group were aware that the above came about from the mapping

$$(x, y) \ddagger (x - 2[x - r], y)$$

A few pupils looked at the sheet on $y = ?$ reflections and then $x + y = ?$ reflections, finding similar results.

Throughout the lessons pupils were absorbed by the task and were keen to communicate their ideas, which is often a problem in Maths. They progressed from the familiar concept of reflection to forming algebraic relationships and finally justifying why these worked. Using the scroll bar in Excel gave them the tool to explore their ideas, with immediate results.

These applied ideas further illustrate the use of ICT as a stimulant for an understanding of ideas which have traditionally been difficult to develop; number patterns and algebra have been around since before the introduction of the computer but there have always been problems in getting students to understand connections (as opposed to reiterating what has been given during the lesson) and take these connections further as a result of a well thought through environment, in this case, integrated ICT and Maths.

ICT within Modern Foreign Languages: Hazel Bailey's work at Turnford School

Elements of ICT within MFL: Turnford School
At Turnford, Hazel Bailey has developed an integrated approach to the use of ICT within her department. The following illustrates her approach and suggests that it should be achieved in a piecemeal manner, that is, built up gradually to include all MFL staff. This case study includes a

range of ICT activities and I have included them with the range of detail given through her own staff development sessions for her department. Both the ICT and MFL National Curricula can be specifically mapped to this work. The general statement in the ICT National Curriculum illustrates this MFL approach:

> During Key Stage three, pupils become increasingly independent users of ICT tools and information sources. They have a better understanding of how ICT can help their work in other subjects and develop their ability to judge when and how to use ICT and where it has limitations. They think about the quality and reliability of information, and access and combine increasing amounts of information. They become more focused, efficient and rigorous in their use of ICT, and carry out a range of increasingly complex tasks.
>
> (DfEE 1999b: 20)

The MFL National Curriculum states, through developing cultural awareness, that pupils should be taught about different countries and cultures by:

- working with authentic materials in the target language, including some from ICT-based sources (for example, handwritten texts, newspapers, magazines, books, video, satellite television, texts from the Internet)
- communicating with native speakers (for example, in person, by correspondence).

(DfEE 1999c: 17)

Hazel Bailey's rationale is as follows:

- introduce ICT gradually, a class at a time
- enrol the help of your school's ICT coordinator
- start with modest tasks and gradually build up.

Word-processing software is the most used application across the whole of education and this can often provide a good base; also, the majority of students will be familiar with the main skills elements of standard applications.

Word-processing project

An ongoing word-processing project is the ideal way to consolidate the basic concepts of any beginner's MFL course, culminating in a professional looking and perfect piece of very personal target language work for every pupil. In many schools this can be achieved by taking students into the ICT room to start the work. With increasing numbers of students having access to PCs at home, or able to use school facilities during the lunch-hour or after school, this will also become an ideal and relevant homework activity.

The content

At various stages during the year, students word process personal items of information in the target language under the heading of 'My family and I' or 'My family, my friends and I'. At each stage the work is printed out, marked, corrected at source by the pupil, and saved on a floppy disk ready for the next stage. By the end of the year the result should be evidence of students working at particular levels and every pupil will have a professional looking piece of target language work about themselves available on disk for future use: it can be printed out and displayed and later filed as National Curriculum evidence; it could be emailed to a friend or sent to the Equipe Online web site: http://www1.oup.co.uk/equipe/equipe2/index.htm. (see Figure 5.4). This is one of several web sites which encourage the sharing of ideas and cultures and exemplify an excellent use of ICT within MFL.

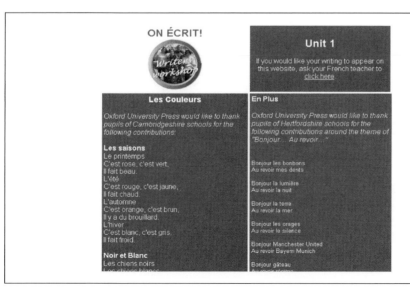

Figure 5.4:   A screen from the Equipe Online web site

ICT skills needed

This is where you liaise with your school's ICT coordinator to find out whether your project will dovetail with skills your students are being taught in their ICT lessons. Of course, many students will already have word-processing skills, but there are other aspects you will need to consider:

- Should all students use the same word-processing package?
- Do all students have a floppy disk?
- Do all students know how to save work to a floppy and know how to store their floppy to prevent damage to the disk?
- Should you suggest that all students double space or 1.5-space their work so that *you* have space to get among the print with your red pen if necessary? If so, do they know how to do this properly without using the space bar?
- Apart from the final printout it may be advisable to prescribe the font and font size (e.g. Times New Roman size 12). This will avoid problems with fonts which do not recognise accents and special characters. It will also avoid problems when transferring work from one computer to another which doesn't have the same range of fonts.
- For the final printout students could change the font and font size provided the accents and special characters are still recognised. Do they know how to highlight the whole text and change it?
- Do students know how to find all the accents and special characters they need?
- Does the school have any foreign language spell checkers? If not, might it be worthwhile getting one?
- Should every draft be labelled (e.g. First Draft, Second Draft etc.) and dated before being printed out?
- Do you want a standardised by-line at the bottom of every pupil's piece of work?
- Could students include clip art, scanned-in images or digital photographs at various stages? If so, do they know how to do this?
- Are students going to file their marked printouts of drafts after each stage?

Suggested stages

Clearly this will vary according to the coursebook you are using, but it could look something like this:

- **Stage 1** Personal details, e.g. name, age, birthday, where you live
- **Stage 2** Physical details, e.g. size, eye colour, hair (colour, length etc.), personality
- **Stage 3** Likes and dislikes

So far this has all been first person singular. Now introduce the third person singular:

- **Stage 4** Family details, e.g. parents, brothers and sisters, pets
- **Stage 5** More detailed information about one parent, one sibling and one pet, including all the information from Stages 1–3 above. This is a lengthy piece of work, but should be within the capabilities of every student if they use their coursebook carefully. There is also scope for differentiation here by content and outcome
- **Stage 6** Home and local area

Adapting the project theme

Quite clearly this kind of project can be adapted for other topics and year groups. Students wishing to continue towards GCSE, for example, can build up a file of personal information throughout their course on all the main topic areas. If marked and subsequently corrected at every stage, such a project forms an excellent base for revision for the final exam. Although some students will dwell on the inconvenience of gaining access to ICT facilities or the slowness of their word-processing skills, they do eventually see the benefit of having work which is easy to correct and which then looks very professional. It does pay off in the end. The drafting and redrafting process is an important part of any composition and, of course, has applications across all curriculum subjects.

Figure 5.5 is an example of the draft stages of the Year 7 project described above. You can clearly see how the work has developed during the drafts.

First Draft

Moi

Je m'appelle Paul. J'ai douze ans. Mon anniversaire est le 5 avril. J'habite à Newby en Angleterre.

DE Paul Jones
15 octobre 2001

Third Draft

Moi

Je m'appelle Paul. J'ai douze ans. Mon anniversaire est le 5 avril. J'habite à Newby en Angleterre. J'ai les yeux verts et les cheveux courts, raides et roux. Je suis assez grand et mince. Je suis très sportif, et assez travailleur. Je suis aussi bavard et marrant.

J'adore le sport: j'aime jouer au foot et au basketball et j'aime la natation. J'aime regarder la télé et aller au fast-food avec mes copains. J'aime aussi faire du vélo et jouer à l'ordinateur. Je n'aime pas aller en ville avec mes parents et je n'aime pas faire du skateboard. Je deteste laver la vaisselle et ranger ma chambre.

DE Paul Jones
10 Décembre 2001

The final draft incorporated graphics as well as text and it is clear to see considerable language skill development from the first draft of the work.

Final Draft

Ma Famille et Moi

Je m'appelle Paul. J'ai douze ans. Mon anniversaire est le 5 avril. J'habite à Newby en Angleterre. J'ai les yeux verts et les cheveux courts, raides et roux. Je suis assez grand et mince. Je suis très sportif, et assez travailleur. Je suis aussi bavard et marrant.

J'adore le sport: j'aime jouer au foot et au basketball et j'aime la natation. J'aime regarder la télé et aller au fast-food avec mes copains. J'aime aussi faire du vélo et jouer à l'ordinateur. Je n'aime pas aller en ville avec mes parents et je n'aime pas faire du skateboard. Je deteste laver la vaisselle et ranger ma chambre.

 Il y a cinq personnes dans ma famille: mon père, ma mère, mes deux soeurs et moi. Mon père s'appelle Chris, ma mère s'appelle Sue, et j'ai deux soeurs qui s'appellent Sophie et Emma. J'ai un chien qui s'appelle Bulldozer et un hamster qui s'appelle Fluffbag.

Ma mère a trente-quatre ans et elle est assez petite et mince. Elle a les yeux bruns et les cheveux mi-longs, raides et châtains. Elle est travailleuse et bavarde. Elle aime lire et se promener avec le chien.

Mon chien s'appelle Bulldozer. Il a 5 ans. Bulldozer a les yeux bruns et les cheveux courts et noirs. Il est assez grand et gros. Il est marrant, maladroit et un peu parresseux. Bulldozer aime manger et regarder la télé. Il n'aime pas faire des promenades dans le jardin public. Il deteste mon hamster!

 J'habite une petite maison en ville. La maison a trois chambres, une cuisine, une salle à manger, un salon et une salle de bains. Il y a un petit jardin derrière la maison. J'habite à Newby dans le sud-est de l'Angleterre. Newby est une petite ville. Dans la ville il y a deux églises, un grand supermarché, des magasins et un centre sportif.

De Paul Jones
22 décembre 2001

Figure 5.5 Drafting stages of producing an MFL word-processed document about 'My family and I'

Desktop publishing and the production of leaflets, posters, brochures and a newspaper

Desktop publishing is a variation and extension of the word-processing project described above. Once students can word process and import images and once they have learnt how to use a DTP package such as Publisher there is no end to the MFL topics which can be developed in the form of a leaflet, flier, brochure or newspaper. For example:

- a leaflet advertising the place where you live
- a brochure advertising your ideal hotel
- a newsletter about your group's holidays (holiday plans in the future tense/holidays they have just had in the past tense)
- a group newsletter about your school incorporating different aspects produced by various members of the group
- posters/fliers about environmental issues.

The planning and design of the DTP pages need careful thought and discussion and this is where the ICT specialist can help: there are certain protocols that should be followed in the design of a leaflet and it is important that these are referenced in some way before the work begins. An important starting point here for the MFL specialist is to refer to the ICT work already undertaken by the group through the assessment and recording procedures in place in the school.

Email project

A good way to learn a foreign language is to use it authentically. We no longer have to rely on costly home-stay visits and exchanges, or the slow process of sending letters to penpals via the post; we can email them direct and receive a swift reply. This is very motivating for MFL students as virtually instant dialogue can take place with native speakers of the language. This can be followed up in the home, particularly as many students now have remote access to computers and are already quite familiar with the processes involved in electronic communication.

As a MFL teacher, you need a link in a target language school. The chances are, if your language degree is not so far behind you, you may already have a link with a school in your target language country. If not, you will need to contact the Central Bureau for Educational Exchanges to see if it can put you in touch with a school for an electronic exchange.

Points to think about when considering an email exchange

- Do all your students have an email address? If not, can they get one through school? If not, explain how to get a free one, for example, through Hotmail or other web-based sources which can be accessed through any computer with Internet access.

- Get a list of email addresses from your target language school.
- Avoid giving each pupil one target language school pupil's email address. It can be demoralising if they don't reply. Give each pupil three addresses: the chances are at least one of these three will prove to be a keen correspondent.
- Remember to teach how to get the accents/special characters using the number pad.
- Encourage the email-literate students to help the not so literate. They soon learn from each other.
- The first email message could be a homework exercise, with blind copies being sent to *your* email address. These can be marked and graded, and you have proof that the message has been sent.
- Encourage your students to forward the first few replies to you. It can be encouraging and motivating for you, too, to see how the link develops.
- Remember that not all students are keen letter writers. Set a new message as a homework task at regular intervals, when they have finished a suitable new topic to write about and to ask questions about.
- Decide whether you need to make any ruling about which language is used for writing messages. A mixture of both is mutually helpful.
- Information gathered from an electronic exchange can be the subject for a group newspaper.
- Electronic exchanges don't have to last for ever, but if they do, then the benefits are legion!

The obvious extension to an electronic exchange is to chat or to participate in a video conferencing session. The software to support this is available on the web and as straightforward as using email. Things to think about:

- First try it out yourself with the link teacher in the target language school.
- Don't forget the time difference when arranging a mutual time.
- Choose a suitable group of students to do this project with: do they have enough language at their finger tips? Are their keyboarding skills fast enough?
- Structure the session: what are they going to chat about? Prepare plenty of questions in advance.
- Decide whether you want any follow-up from the session, and if so, in what format.

And finally...
There are many resources available for the teaching of MFL. If you want to look at MFL specific software then consider the following:

- Find out what is available at your school and familiarise yourself with it
- Visit other schools to familiarise yourself with and to evaluate their software
- If given a budget to buy some software, don't forget to include the price of the site licence (often considerably more than the actual software itself).

A useful starting point for a web-based resource is the site set up by the Scottish Centre for Information on Language Teaching and Research (CILT) at www.linguaweb.co.uk

Choosing an appropriate application for the job

Having looked at various Key Stage 3 applications, there are issues that need looking at before choosing which software application is to be used for a particular project. This is even more important when using open-ended software such as a spreadsheet and the work at Penrice Community College illustrates an application that would be difficult to achieve in anything other than a spreadsheet. An understanding of the appropriate use of an application is important and should form part of the planning and discussion associated with ICT-based work throughout all key stages.

For example, students working at level 7 need to show that 'they identify the advantages and limitations of different information handling applications. They select and use information systems suited to their work in a variety of contexts'. If you are working on a project which is essentially numerical, then a spreadsheet may satisfy the requirements of the project more than a database, which has more administration associated with it in the form of field design, etc. The same can be the case when designing a school newspaper. Is it better to use a word processor or a desktop publishing application? The difference between the two is now blurred but historically, the distinction between the two was clear; word processing was used as a means for creating text and this would ultimately be inserted into a DTP application along with graphics and clip art (created in a graphics application). Now, many ICT users use the DTP application to produce all the material. Also, modern word processors have facilities beyond the DTP applications of a few years ago.

Common ICT misconceptions

Whatever subject you teach, if you are using ICT within it then you need to be aware of the ICT concepts and understanding that students bring with them to your subject. There are two common elements to using ICT across the curriculum:

- all tasks involve students interacting with an operating system, usually Windows
- all tasks involve the use of a software application.

Once the most appropriate application has been chosen, mistakes are bound to happen and although some mistakes are difficult to spot, there may be a commonality to the way different students react to the same situation. For example, when using the web, many students double click on hot spots when a single click will suffice. The result may be the same but the outcome may have been achieved through a *misconception*: you double-click to load an application but single-click to activate a hot spot.

What common misconceptions are there? Here are three examples:

- Students who do not understand the function of a word wrap using a word processor; they carefully watch the screen as they move towards the end of the line and when they think that the next word they are going to type will not fit in, they press the return key.
- Students who, when saving a file in an application, cannot find it for subsequent editing as it is saved in an unknown location. Also, the saving of an edited file in the same location it originated from instead of saving it on, say, a floppy disk (involving navigation through Windows) for use on a different computer.
- When using a spreadsheet, some students always use a function even if they are adding the values in two cells. For example, entering =SUM(a1+a2) adds the two values together even though SUM is meant to add a range of numbers. There is no feedback to let the students know that the function is not needed.

As a new subject to the curriculum, there is no history to common misconceptions as there are in established subjects such as Maths and English. As new applications develop then along with them come a range of misconceptions when the application is used. In the example above, you may have thought of the use of the web, say through using a search engine; this can throw up misconceptions like the entering of a **uniform resource location** (URL) in the search criteria. It could also be argued that not using an established bookmark facility is a misconception. Of course, all of the above may not be misconceptions; they may be acts done out of choice. This is highlighted through the many ways it is possible to perform the same function. When using a word processor, there are many shortcuts to items contained on the pull-down menus, for example, cutting text, printing and saving work. Is it a misconception to use a menu rather than a shortcut? How do you know that a student is aware of the many different ways of achieving the same end result? Looking at a range of students may give you some interesting results. For example, many students do the following out of choice:

- They use SAVE AS instead of SAVE within an application because they think that the two functions serve the same purpose.
- They delete back to a spelling mistake to correct it and then have to retype what has been deleted. Few students leave corrections until the end.
- Some use the caps lock key to type a capital rather than the shift key.

You could argue that these are misconceptions and in some cases, they will be, but not in all cases. To establish why a certain act is done can happen only following a discussion with the student.

Summary

In this chapter, I have discussed the structure and implementation of two specific models of ICT delivery (discrete and integrated) and related them to practical examples of implementation. The background to ICT delivery at Key Stage 3 has its roots firmly in the broader area of introducing an innovation and the way innovation is disseminated in schools.

ICT can support all curriculum areas and I have specifically discussed the use in Maths and Modern Foreign Languages. Even though one of the Maths examples has been long established, it is important that the context of delivery is clear to students and in this case, the school is working from an integrated ICT model which ensures that the ICT coordinator has involvement from another department. The ICT coordinator's role is mainly one of staff development in that he was not involved in the delivery of the module.

The MFL example is similar in that the MFL department is responsible for the ICT component throughout Key Stage 3. This approach is moving towards multiple integration where the MFL department may become a centre in its own right and could then have other departments at its periphery, for example, having an input in MFL departments in other schools.

As ICT skills develop, it is possible to see how students make common mistakes and misconceptions about what many of us consider to be basic ICT methods and processes. It is important to identify these as they occur and it is often difficult to agree what a misconception is. Sometimes students use ICT in a particular way out of choice and not because of a misconception.

References

Crawford, R. (1997) *Managing Information Technology in Secondary Schools*. London: Routledge.

DfEE (1998) *A Review of Secondary Education Schools in England*. London: HMSO.

DfEE (1999a) *Mathematics, The National Curriculum for England, Key Stages 1–4*. London: DfEE.

DfEE (1999b) *Information and Communication Technology, The National Curriculum for England, Key Stages 1–4*. London: DfEE.

DfEE (1999c) *Modern Foreign Languages, The National Curriculum for England, Key Stages 3–4*. London: DfEE.

Mulkerrins, P. (2000) 'Scroll bars in Excel', *Micromath*, Summer Association for Teachers of Mathematics, 16(2), 24–7.

Papert, S. (1993) *Mindstorms. Children, Computers and Powerful Ideas*, 2nd edn. London: The Harvester-Wheatsheaf.

Schon, D. A. (1971) *Beyond the Stable State: Public and Private Learning in a Changing Society*. London: Temple Smith.

CHAPTER 6

The assessment of ICT at Key Stage 3

The objectives of this chapter are as follows:

- To discuss the issues related to the assessment, recording and reporting of ICT capability with particular reference to Key Stage 3
- To investigate a range of approaches to ICT assessment currently taking place in schools.

The assessment of ICT capability is an essential element of the teaching and learning process: if assessments are not done regularly then future planning will not be tailored to the needs of the students. This chapter investigates the structure of ICT assessment as laid down in the National Curriculum and looks at practical methods of levelling against the attainment target criteria discussed through the **level descriptions**. The schools discussed in this chapter approach the assessment process in a realistic manner and employ practical approaches to both formative and summative assessments. Key to this chapter is the notion of formative assessment and the value of regular feedback to make the final levelling process much easier than a one-off assessment.

ICT assessment and the National Curriculum

The one attainment target for ICT has eight level descriptions and one for exceptional performance. The statutory requirement to report a level at the end of Key Stage 3 should ideally involve the tracking of performance over a three-year period culminating in the attributing of a level, informed from what has come before. The way that this is done depends on the ICT organisation and delivery within the school in that where a school operates a discrete ICT delivery model, it may be that the ICT coordinator has sole responsibility for this. Alternatively, inherent in the cross-curricular approach is the assessment of elements of ICT capability within the other curriculum subjects. This can lead to inconsistency of assessment but at least more than one teacher can be involved in the process. Many sentences in the level descriptions refer to the use of ICT in context and this can often be judged more accurately from within the 'context', i.e. another subject area. For example, level 7 states:

> They select and use information systems suited to their work in a variety of contexts, translating inquiries expressed in ordinary language into the form required by the system… They take part in informed discussions about the social, economic, ethical and moral issues raised by ICT.

Assessment of the above could be possible within most curriculum subjects where ICT is used.

When students start secondary education, they bring with them a level attributed from the primary school and it is important that the ICT coordinator has a feel for how this was arrived at. Easy to say, difficult to do! Secondary schools have many primary feeder schools and it is virtually impossible to know what is happening in all of them. A starting point is for the coordinator to visit primary schools during the Summer term to establish what is taking place in the form of teaching and assessment. Many primary schools now have computer labs and along with this often comes a structure quite similar to discrete ICT delivery at Key Stage 3.

Another approach to providing an informed ICT curriculum in Year 7 is to let the primary schools know what is expected of students at the primary – secondary transfer stage. This could consist of a generic document sent out to schools and along with this guidance could come a primary ICT curriculum outline of work to be covered. Even though this does not include student differentiation it can still provide a starting point for discussions between the primary and secondary teachers responsible for this link. Discrete ICT delivery in Year 7 often involves students being set according to ability in another subject, or by form, so a mixed ability ICT class is the norm.

The levels

The levels can be found at the back of the ICT National Curriculum document or from the web site at www.nc.uk.net. At the beginning of Year 7, students should be within the level range 3–7.

It is a difficult process to attribute an ICT level to a student. Whichever level is awarded, the assessor needs to ensure that this is clearly distinguished between the level below and the level above the one attributed. For example, the level 6 and 7 descriptions are as follows:

Level 6
Pupils develop and refine their work to enhance its quality, using information from a range of sources. Where necessary, they use complex lines of enquiry to test hypotheses. They present their ideas in a variety of ways and show a clear sense of audience. They develop, try out and refine sequences of instructions to monitor, measure and control events, and show efficiency in framing these instructions. They use ICT-based models to make predictions and vary the rules within the models. They assess the validity of these models by comparing their behaviour with information from other sources. They discuss the impact of ICT on society.

Level 7
Pupils combine information from a variety of ICT-based and other sources for presentation to different audiences. They identify the advantages and limitations of different information-handling applications. They select and use information systems suited to their work in a variety of contexts, translating enquiries expressed in ordinary language into the form required by the system. They use ICT to measure, record and analyse physical variables and control events. They design ICT-based models and procedures with variables to meet particular needs. They consider the benefits and limitations of ICT tools and information sources and of the results they produce, and they use these results to inform future judgments about the quality of their work. They take part in informed discussions about the use of ICT and its impact on society.

Activity 6.1
List the key differences that would exemplify a piece of work attributed at level 7 rather than level 6.

This activity has probably illustrated the difficulties involved in levelling. There are many student levels attributed that could go either way depending upon who is accrediting the work and there is an obvious directive role here for the ICT coordinator. A key distinction between levels 6 and 7 is related to the application used for the purpose: an example of this could be the use of a standard data-handling package (i.e. a database) rather than a spreadsheet. Of course, a spreadsheet application is used for data handling but there will be examples of using Excel, say, for a project dealing with many numerical calculations which is much more appropriate than using Access, which has different features. It is important that the student clearly articulates why the chosen application is being used. Also, a level 7 student should be able to integrate data between applications ('Pupils combine information from a variety of ICT-based and other sources for presentation to different audiences'), for example, exporting data from a database into a spreadsheet in order to carry out calculations. Such integrated work will need to be discussed and documented in the project to exemplify level 7, rather than level 6.

Level partitioning: the Manton School

A crucial element to the accurate reporting of a level is that all the criteria need to be achieved. If a student has achieved 90 per cent of a level then he/she is, in real terms, *working towards* that level. Assessing through a single project makes it more difficult to level accurately and the best examples of levelling tend to come from schools that have a range of broad assignments completed regularly across the three-year Key Stage 3 period. To do this, there needs to be a recording system in place which maps the level criteria to the work. For example, when an assessor makes an initial judgement at level 6, he/she needs to map the assessed work to the level and taking the level 6 criteria as an example, they could be partitioned as follows:

Level 6
6.1 Develop and refine work
6.2 Use information from a range of sources
6.3 Where necessary, hypotheses testing
6.4 Ideas presented in a variety of ways
6.5 Monitor, measure and control events
6.6 Use ICT-based models to make predictions
6.7 Assess these models against other sources
6.8 Discuss the impact of ICT on society.

The Manton School has devised grids to map ICT assessment to core subjects. An assessment grid for level 6 which tracks individual performance through different assignments is illustrated here.

Level 6 criteria map

	En	Ma	Sc	ICT
6.1	✔			✔
6.2	✔	✔	✔	
6.3		✔	✔	✔
6.4	✔	✔	✔	✔
6.5		✔	✔	✔
6.6		✔	✔	✔
6.7				✔
6.8	✔			✔

Each ticked cell refers to an element of the partition being covered and assessed (no matter how brief) in some form within a core subject. There is a table for each partitioned level and an individual overall assessment at level 6 (in this case) needs the student to provide evidence to support the level. As each piece of work is being assessed, the criterion number (e.g. 6.2) would be inserted into the assignment at the place where it is exemplified and this makes the mapping easier for the student and the teacher. Implicit in this approach is *student self-assessment* where students are responsible for *claiming* that their work is at a certain level. Self-assessment is a Year 9 activity and through this kind of structure, development over the whole of Key Stage 3 can be monitored. Each criterion suggests that they are able to offer ICT support in the ticked areas and this is made easier through the setting across the core subjects: students in the top set for Maths in Year 8, in this example, are expected to work towards level 6 by the end of the year and those who are working at a different level will be using the appropriate level grid.

Of course, the above example relies upon an approach which has a cross-curricular element and as can be seen from the grid, there is a discrete element through the subject ICT being included. Criterion 6.5 is integrated into Science through data logging, Maths through discrete Logo and in ICT through the use of Lego control software although this is soon to be delivered within Design and Technology. As foundation subjects gradually use ICT then the grid will be extended to include these developments.

There are issues to do with consistency of assessment in this approach in that several members of staff are responsible for providing levels for their itemised work at the end of each academic year. This has to come with evidence and the ultimate level awarded is as a result of moderation with the ICT coordinator.

A crucial element to the use of ICT at Key Stage 3 is the ability of students to work as autonomous learners. There are implications for access to ICT equipment if this is to be achieved and it is important that this is recognised in the planning of ICT: students need access to hardware and software outside the timetable, through after school/lunch-time clubs, access before the start of school and at the end of school. If this access is monitored, there is no reason why autonomous project work should not be developed. The Manton School provides out-of-school access through various clubs both before and after school.

ICT assessment: Kingsford Community School

Kingsford was opened in 2000 and at time of writing has Years 7 and 8 only. The ICT coordinator has the responsibility for ensuring that a rigid ICT assessment policy is in place. Of course, he can do this gradually as the school fills up over a five-year period but he is aware that a generic assessment structure is key and that this can evolve along with the growth of the school.

The starting point for accurate assessment is the primary school. The ICT coordinator has a timetabled slot in the Summer term when he visits feeder primary schools and talks to primary teachers and students and gets a feel for the ICT support given. This may not be totally accurate as there are many feeder schools but it forms the starting point for Year 7 ICT, which consists of a primary–secondary transfer introductory project, designed to introduce students to the school. The work is done during the first half-term of Year 7 and although there will be activities which overlap the primary phase, the school still gains useful information regarding ICT skills in particular. An extract from the project is illustrated in Table 6.1.

Year 7 Mini Project

- The main purpose of this project is to make students from primary school feel better about the move from primary school to secondary school. To achieve this we need to know your experiences so far so that we can pass them back to your primary school.
- At the end of the project, when you have finished everything, we will send some of the projects off to the primary schools so that their children can read it.
- This project will take us up to half term. This means you have plenty of time to complete it and create the best possible project.

Part 1: Front Cover
It is important for you all to create a front cover for your work. Your front cover must have the following information on it.
Title: Coming to Kingsford Community School
Subtitle: The Truth about Moving from Primary School to Secondary School
Name: Your name has to be on the front cover.
Tutor group: Your tutor group should be on the front cover.
Name of primary school: The name of your primary school should be on the front cover.

Part 2: Introduction
In this introduction you are going to tell the students from the primary school a little about your experiences when making the move from one school to another.

This section should include the following, and have the following headings for each part:

Heading 1: Fears
In this section you should write about what you were scared or worried about before you came to Kingsford Community School.

You should also say why you were worried. You could also say if anyone helped you to get over these worries.

Heading 2: What I was Excited about
In this section you should write about the things you were excited about and why.

Heading 3: First Impressions
In this section you should talk about your first impressions of Kingsford Community School (this should not be about your first day). You could talk about what you had heard about the school or any taster days you had attended. You could write about summer school if you attended this.

You could also write about what the school looked like and the things your parents/carers had told you about it.

Heading 4: First Day at Kingsford Community School
In this section you should write about your first day at Kingsford; try include the following:

The teachers and head teacher
Friends
What happened?
Were you scared?
Your tutor group

Table 6.1   An introductory ICT-based project at Kingsford Community School

The project extends to a class survey and all students gain experience of using Office in an integrated way. The ICT coordinator looks upon these as baseline skills needed for the development of further ICT skills.

Kingsford has designed its own units which make up discrete ICT delivery at Key Stage 3 and consist of the following:

* Unit 1 An introduction to ICT
* Unit 2 An introduction to Word
* Unit 3 Mini project
* Unit 4 The Internet
* Unit 5 An introduction to spreadsheets

Each unit is assessed upon its completion and the student plays a part in this. Each student has an interview with an ICT teacher and has to show that he/she understands each of the criteria either by discussion or with evidence.

One pupil, Mustafa, documented his progress in the spreadsheet unit as follows; this went towards the final end-of-unit report.

I can use information from a questionnaire in a spreadsheet to produce charts and find totals.

Using these charts I can tell others what the information means and also understand how realistic my findings are.

I understand that poor quality information can produce useless results.

I can copy and paste information from a variety of sources (Internet) into different work, such as a word processor or a spreadsheet.

I can present my work in different ways depending on who I am showing it to.

I can use the computer to explore patterns and relationships.

I can use a spreadsheet to predict what will happen if I change data.

I can compare how we use ICT in school to how it is used out of school.

There are three formal assessment periods during the year where progress is reported to parents and it is the unit assessments which inform each of the three summative assessments. The reporting procedure takes the form of an academic progress file as illustrated in Table 6.2.

Mustafa   Mohammed
E = Effort **A** = Achievement **N/C** = National Curriculum Level

Subject	Level Achieved			Comment
	E	**A**	**N/C**	
Art				
Design and Technology				
English				
French				
Geography				
History				
ICT	B	B	3/4	Mustafa has made good progress in ICT. He has shown a good understanding of the Internet and Ms Word and has given evidence showing an improvement from the previous assessment. He needs to concentrate at all times if he is to achieve a level 4 by the end of the term.
Life Skills				
Maths				
Mandarin				
Music				
Physical Education				
Religious Education				
Science				

Table 6.2   Example of an academic progress profile

As this levelling exercise is done formatively throughout the Key Stage 3 years, the ICT coordinator has highlighted problems attributing a level even though it is informed from much evidence:

We have a commitment to report levels to children and their parents through each of the three assessment points and we find it difficult to get enough evidence together to clearly state that a child has achieved level 3, say. We could just give a level 2 but in many cases, that would not give the whole picture. So what we shall do for next year is to break each level into 3 parts, lower, middle and higher. 3L (lower) indicates that the child has definitely achieved level 2 and has given evidence to show that level 3 is being worked on and the child has achieved some of the criteria. A few more criteria would result in a report at level 3M (middle). By the time we have the complete Key Stage 3 age range in the school, we will have enough evidence for an end of key stage assessment which is accurate and can be justified with evidence.

This sounds like a realistic approach to assessment and is achieved because of the formative way it is done, levels being focused on at non-statutory reporting times which will ultimately inform the end of Key Stage 3 assessment. The units included are for Year 7 only at this stage and are to be extended through to Year 9 as ICT will continue to be delivered in a discrete manner for the purposes of assessment.

ICT Year 9 project: Epping St John's School
ICT is delivered discretely at St John's School and a Year 9 project contributes towards the summative level. This is a particularly useful project because it contributes towards the GCSE ICT being delivered at Key Stage 4 and is picked up at the beginning of Year 10.

Students have to produce a folder containing a project which has several elements included. Carmen explains the project:

In this project, I have worked with Louise and we have created our own business which is a nightclub called West Club 2000. We named our club like this because it will open in the new year of 2000 and it is based in Holborn, London. We have produced questionnaires and given them to people to fill in. We have designed and printed tickets for the club and we have written a conclusion to the whole project.

We have also included business essentials such as a stock inventory, application forms and employee profiles. We have designed our club for over 18s and have employed bouncers for this reason. The results of the questionnaire suggest that we should have a live DJ and not basic pop music.

The two students included the questionnaire design and results in their folder and clearly distinguished which one was responsible for which part. They distinguished between the flier, which was designed to be displayed on notice boards, and the newspaper advert, including the different audiences each was supposed to attract. Also, they produced staff badges, which are easy to read, headed notepaper and a business card for employees.

The project involved considerable design work and a discussion of the context of the different elements involved. Along with this was the setting up of the questionnaire in a spreadsheet, tailoring the spreadsheet to make analysis useful for further project planning. They took the results of the first questionnaire, interpreted them and then contacted several other clubs to see if there was a generic element to their findings:

From the results of the questionnaire, it was clear to see that people wanted snacks to be available on the club premises. We have done more research to find out what other clubs and some small pubs sell as snacks. A club in Ilford sells all kinds of Asian food such as spicy hot chicken wings, lamb and chicken curry, chicken tikka as well as crisps and more luxurious food.

The Sphinx Bar is nearby and it is split into two, half is designed for the general public and the other half is rented out for hire. They sell spring rolls, sausage rolls, pasties and different types of salad, sandwiches and chips. Using this information, I will produce a suitable menu for our customers.

Finally, they produced a discussion about the use of ICT as an overall tool in preparing the club for opening. An overall level 6 was awarded for both of these students as they had integrated the use of ICT into a practical situation and justified the level through discussions with the ICT coordinator.

The QCA schemes of work

The QCA has developed schemes of work for each curriculum subject to aid the delivery process, particularly with recent (2000) developments in the National Curriculum. Many schools are now using these schemes in various forms and as they stand, they are more suited to use in a discrete delivery model: for them to be used in a cross-curricular manner, elements (known as units) would need to be developed through the different subjects. The following case study looks at the assessment procedure for the work discussed in Chapter 5.

A further partitioning example: Davenant Foundation School
Davenant Foundation School's use of the QCA schemes of work has been discussed in Chapter 5. By the end of Year 9, students will have covered the units and the final end of key stage level will be attributed as a result of analysis of all the previous levels given over the three-year period. For example, a level given in Year 7 should have been improved on by completing subsequent units and there should be an element of progression visible in a student progress file.

The mark scheme for Unit 3, Processing text and images, has been constructed with levels in mind: you can see in Table 6.3 that there are distinguishing features at each level. For example, a distinction between levels 4 and 5 is in the processing of scanned images as well as *developing* a range of templates rather than *using* a template.

Level	Mark	Students will produce
6	18–20	• A newspaper which has been produced collectively in pairs or groups • A process of newspaper production • Develop a range of template styles for a variety of uses • Use the templates to produce different pages • Evidence that they understand the difference between a document and a template • Scan suitable images from identified sources • Process images • Present text in an appropriate way • Use Spell Check

		• Use a range of colours and styles which are appropriate to the newspaper style and the audience.
5	**16–17**	• A newspaper which has been produced collectively in pairs or groups • Develop a range of template styles for a variety of uses • Use the templates to produce different pages • Evidence that they understand the difference between a document and a template • Scan suitable images from identified sources • Process images • Present text in an appropriate way • Use Spell Check • Use a range of colours and styles which are appropriate to the newspaper style and the audience.
4	**14–15**	• A newspaper which has been produced collectively in pairs or groups • Use the template to produce different pages • Evidence that they understand the difference between a document and a template • Scan suitable images from identified sources • Present text in an appropriate way • Use Spell Check • Use a range of colours and styles which are appropriate to the newspaper style and the audience.

3	12–13	• A newspaper which has been produced collectively in pairs or groups • Use the template to produce different pages • Scan suitable images from identified sources • Use Spell Check • Use a range of colours and styles which are appropriate to the newspaper style and the audience.
2	9–11	• A newspaper which has been produced collectively in pairs or groups • Scan suitable images from identified sources • Use Spell Check
1	0–8	• A newspaper which has been produced collectively in pairs or groups • Use Spell Check

Table 6.3   Year 7 Unit 3 Processing Text and Images: levelling criteria at Davenant Foundation School

Breaking up the level descriptions in this way is a time-consuming process but is necessary if you want to map them to the work of the unit. Once all the unit assessments have been mapped to the level descriptions, then it is possible to level a student accurately. Also, you can see the flexibility of including a small mark range within each level. This ensures a fair spread between students.

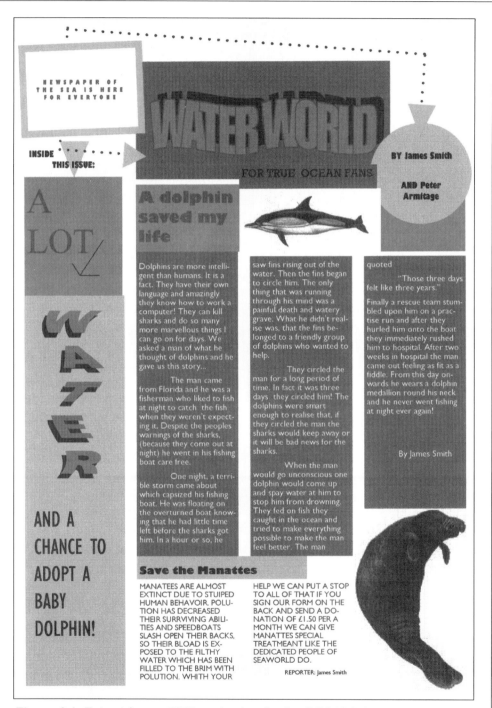

Figure 6.1 Extract from a DTP production for the QCA Unit 3

A group of three students produced a newspaper, an extract from which is illustrated in Figure 6.1. They were all accredited at level 6. This level was awarded followed discussions between the students and the ICT teacher along with formative assessments as it was under development. Each student had to justify their input in the production under the breakdown criteria detailed in Table 6.3.

Summary

In this chapter, I have discussed the practical approaches used by four schools to assess ICT capability accurately at the end of Key Stage 3. There are some common threads to assessment between the schools discussed, for example, the breaking down of levels into manageable, assessable components and assessing across Years 7, 8 and 9. The most important ingredient of accurate assessment is the accumulation of each student profile across the Key Stage 3 phase so that an ultimate level is not seen as a 'stab in the dark'. Formative assessment is key here and this can be achieved only through a recording procedure that is established on entry to secondary education. Schools assess in different ways but if you are part of this process, then you need to be in a position to justify your reporting.

CHAPTER 7

ICT at Key Stage 4

The objectives of this chapter are as follows:

- To discuss Graphic User Interface design issues and how they follow through to GCSE ICT
- To look at the nature of ICT assessment at Key Stage 4 through the GCSE IT and the new GCSE ICT
- To give examples of assessed work for the project element of the GCSE course.

Graphic User Interface design issues

Whether you are an ICT specialist or teaching ICT within another subject, it is essential that you are aware of the functions and purposes of the interface you are working with and the understanding that students have of the processes they are working through. The Graphic User Interface (GUI, pronounced 'gooey') in front of us can be confusing, often difficult to believe that it has been designed in the first place!

Grange Park School (discussed in Chapter 3) has an ICT awareness programme in Year 10 which builds on the discrete ICT taught throughout Key Stage 3. One unusual element of this course is that it is taught through Design and Technology over a period of three weeks and has **Human–Computer Interaction** (**HCI**, the discipline associated with GUI design) as its focus. This section discusses the elements covered in the brief programme and could provide a useful start for understanding the GUI. There are many screen design issues to consider through the GCSE ICT and an understanding of the principles can help these processes.

It was during the 1980s that Apple produced the Mac, which had one of the first GUI interfaces for the microcomputer. Microsoft then developed the PC alternative in Windows. There have been many developments of the Windows interface, the most important being the flexibility built into Windows 95 as this was much more like the Mac equivalent. Of course, GUI issues do not solely relate to Windows; any software application has a GUI as well and at Grange Park, their starting point is Microsoft Word.

Microsoft Word is a piece of software that is familiar to most. Have a look at Figure 7.1, which is an extract from the standard Word 97 toolbar; can you work out the purpose of each icon? Look particularly at the icons at either end.

Figure 7.1   Extract from the standard Word 97 toolbar

You can see that they are quite similar but refer to quite different functions: the left-most icon refers to the print preview facility which gives you an idea what the document will look like when printed out whereas the right-most icon is a document map, showing you the structure of the document overall, with paragraph headings. The common element to these icons is the magnifying glass (illustrating a focus from above maybe), but this interpretation is obviously subjective.

The Year 10 teacher discussed the meanings of this icon bar with her class (entitled 'ICT awareness') and while many students realised the purpose of most of the icons, they were not aware what the metaphor signified. Metaphor plays an important part in interface design and some designs do a better job than others.

The teacher then continued to discuss the principles of design using the academic terminology associated with HCI. This centred around what makes a good interface and she gave students the criteria for the evaluation of existing interfaces.

Design principles

There is an important educational issue associated with the evaluation of current interfaces: prior to schools buying PC hardware and software, the equipment that they had would have probably been tailored to the education market, and the interaction afforded would be for a specific school audience. This is often not the case now as secondary and upper primary students tend to be thrown in at the deep end with software used and designed for business and commerce. Any kind of interface discussion pertains to use outside of school as well as inside as it is the same software and not a cut-down version.

So what form should an interface critique take? The sizes of icon and font come immediately to mind but these can usually be changed by the user and are quite low level principles when compared to the three main principles of **Affordance**, **Visibility** and **Feedback**.

The affordance of an icon refers to the features (if any) which make it obvious how to use it. For example, an icon which appears raised from the screen seems to want to be pressed; it *affords* to be pressed and so the affordance is good. The *visibility* of a icon refers to the effect of pressing it; is it immediately obvious what has happened? The *feedback* relates to the information sent back to the user regarding the final result of the action.

An example of icon evaluation
Figure 7.2 illustrates an extract from the formatting toolbar from Word. You will probably be quite familiar with these icons and can use them effectively, but have they been designed with the user in mind? How do the bold, italic and underline buttons fare when it comes to affordance, visibility and feedback?

When you move the mouse over the button, it becomes 3D so this does

Figure 7.2   A further extract from the standard Word 97 toolbar

afford to be pressed. As with most software, a description appears telling you that this is the bold button. Affordance is quite good. Visibility is there in that the button appears depressed, i.e. the result of the action is quite obvious. Feedback is a different matter in that the effectiveness of the action depends on what you have done prior to clicking the button; if you have highlighted text then the feedback is good as it becomes emboldened. However, if you are simply pressing the button with no highlighted text selected, then it is not clear at all what has happened. Most of us highlight text first so from this perspective, feedback is good.

Activity 7.1
Comment on the affordance, visibility and feedback in Figure 7.3, with particular reference to:
• the view icons
• the slider bar.

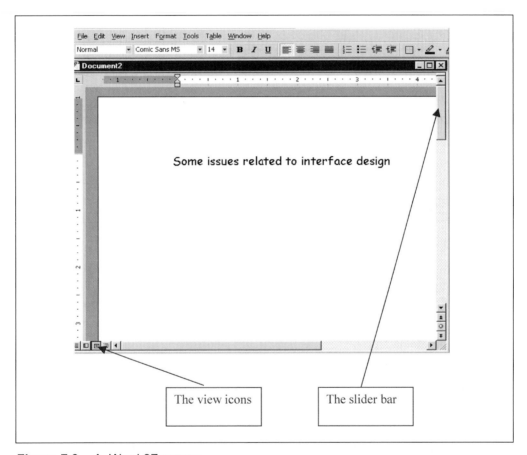

Figure 7.3   A Word 97 screen

Icons are often misinterpreted but once understood, problems disappear. These issues have become more relevant recently because we tend to use a standard range of generic software across all age phases, albeit in different ways. As mentioned previously, Microsoft products were not designed with education in mind; they are business applications which contain features which can take much of the work away from the user. This can be problematic when using the software with students in that it is not always clear what the students have designed themselves; for example, the inclusion of ready made templates which are available in products such as Word and Publisher seems to have taken away the creativity once needed in the production of a high class electronic publication.

Buttons and boxes

Following on from discussions about elements of the standard Word menus, students at Grange Park then investigate the use and appropriateness of check boxes and radio buttons.

Figure 7.4 refers to what is available when selecting options from the toolbar. Check boxes are used here because the user needs the option of selecting more than one box (a facility of check boxes).

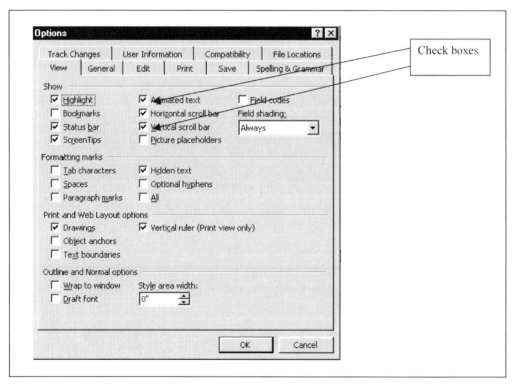

Figure 7.4   Check boxes from the *options* menu: several may be selected

In contrast, Figure 7.5 shows the shutdown window where one radio button is selected (only one selection is possible). In the case illustrated, it would clearly be wrong for a designer to allow multiple selection.

Figure 7.5   The shutdown window: one button only can be selected

Following these examples, students are then encouraged to contrast the two design considerations. They then explore how these issues relate to the design of a questionnaire, for example, selecting male/female (button, only one selection possible), food eaten today (check box, several selections possible), rating on a scale 1 to 5 (button) and which type of music do you like? (check box).

Considering the broader implications of interface design through questionnaires can complement the coursework that has to be produced for the GCSE ICT project work.

Further HCI issues and resources can be found at www.bcs-hci.org.uk

GCSE IT/ICT courses: some key features

Some schools do not offer subject-specific ICT at Key Stage 4 and are only just beginning to look into the requirements of courses offered by examination boards. Ideally, students should be offered a continuum of ICT experiences across the 11–16 age range and a GCSE ICT course should build on the range of work done during Key Stage 3. There is, of course, a statutory requirement to deliver ICT at Key Stage 4 and all examining boards cover the National Curriculum requirements.

Since 2001, all boards have changed the name (and to some extent, the content) of their courses from IT to ICT.

Syllabus requirements vary from board to board but there is still a vast amount of work that is included across them all. The structure of a GCSE course is consistent in terms of assessment in that all boards have a 60 per cent coursework and 40 per cent exam structure. It is important that time is included in the design of the course for students to have a taught, academic component as it is not the case that the theory element will come out of the practical work, as is often suggested by teachers. GCSE ICT teaching needs classroom-based work in the same way as other subjects.

Most boards provide sample exam papers and specimen answers so it is important that these are looked at in relation to the syllabus.

All boards offer the new GCSE ICT in full- and short-course mode; the short course equates to half of one GCSE and can be taken with other short courses. A short course consists of one exam paper and a range of coursework. The full course has an additional paper with further coursework. By way of example, the OCR examining board has the following structure.

OCR examining board
The OCR (Oxford, Cambridge and RSA) examining board (www.ocr.org.uk) suggests in its documentation that there are several ways to deliver the current GCSE:

> The syllabus covers the requirements of the National Curriculum Order 1995 for Information Technology at Key Stage 4 and the GCSE Subject Criteria for Information Technology... The course is designed to be taught either across the curriculum or as a discrete subject.

In schools where the GCSE is offered, it is usually taught as a discrete subject, whether in full- or short-course mode. Schools offering the short course often combine it with another short course such as Business Studies and this can give a breadth of experience to the student and can be counted together with the various full courses studied.

The following discussion refers to the GCSE IT, now superseded by a change in name to ICT, as mentioned above, with a few changes in structure. It is worth updating with the current regulations as they become available.

OCR: the structure of GCSE IT
Students are entered for the GCSE at either the Foundation or Higher Tier. For the short course, students have to take a written paper (which differs between the tiers) counting for 40 per cent of the overall score, and a project which makes up the other 60 per cent. There are two written papers for the full course.

Students have to cover all seven units for the written exam:

- Information Handling
- Communicating
- Measuring
- Control
- Modelling
- System Design
- Application and Effects

Exam questions tend to be short although there is more subject content in the full course, as would be expected. However, this changes for the coursework as students are assessed on two of the first five units only. To achieve this, short-course students can produce one or two pieces of coursework, as long as the criteria are met. The board gives advice on project work and as a school offering the course, you should specify which projects are most suitable.

In addition to the tasks above, full-course students have to undertake further coursework in the form of a major task.

An example of minor tasks: Nick (short course)
These two projects fall neatly into the exemplar materials given by the board; indeed the second project follows the board's communicating material exactly. This is a good way to ensure that you are sticking to the criteria of the board and by offering students a limited range of tasks, this makes standardisation in marking easier. All coursework is marked by the school and moderated by the board.

Nick has produced two pieces of coursework to satisfy the two strands of Information Handling and Communicating.

Information Handling
Following the statement of the problem to be solved, this is broken down into five sections as follows:

1. *Analysis*: how it is done, research and data collection, software and hardware requirements
2. *Design*: document design, database planning sheet, data capture sheet
3. *Implementation*: implementation document, user guide, the database and validation

4. *Testing*: amended printout of database, introduction to testing, sorting, simple and complex searches, questionnaire searches, summary of testing, sample graphs
5. *Evaluation* of the whole process.

He discusses the problem as follows:

For the Information Handling strand of the coursework, I have been asked by a local estate agent to design a database with the basic details of the properties for sale. The system should be designed to help prospective buyers, giving them details of properties for sale. The system should include details of location, price, and number of bedrooms. It should save prospective buyers' time as it should give them, very rapidly, details of any property that closely matches their requirements. They won't have to flick through hundreds of leaflets of properties they don't actually want.

Each part of the project needs to be thoroughly researched. For example, Nick researched what type of information about houses was included in property advertisements from a range of sources. Using these data, he then designed a data capture sheet to include these fields, thus making sure that his database will ultimately have as much information in it as possible. This design phase can take up much time and as with all stages of project work, needs careful monitoring and deadline setting. His research was documented as shown in the box.

Research on different fields for my database
I carried out some research, from four different sources. For each source I found the ten main fields and wrote them down below.

My first piece of research is on a set of details I picked up from a local estate agent.

1. Location
2. Price
3. Number of bedrooms
4. Type of house (detached, terraced, etc.)

5. Position
6. Garage
7. En suite bathroom
8. Central heating
9. Garden
10. Double glazing

My second piece of research is on the property pages, which is from a local newspaper.

1. Price
2. Location
3. Type of house (detached, terraced, etc.)
4. Number of bedrooms
5. Garage
6. Garden
7. Position
8. Age
9. Style (house, flat, bungalow)
10. Swimming pool

My third piece of research was on the questionnaire I carried out.

1. Type of house (detached, terraced, etc.)
2. Number of bedrooms
3. Position
4. Garage
5. Location
6. Garden
7. Price
8. Aspect of house
9. Special requirements (near schools, parks, shops, in a quiet road, etc.)
10. Double glazing

My final piece of research was on a property web site on the Internet.

1. Number of bedrooms
2. Price
3. Type of house (detached, terraced, etc.)
4. Garden
5. Double glazing
6. Position
7. Central Heating
8. Location
9. Garage
10. En suite bathroom

Nick then analysed the results and came up with a representative number of fields to represent house details accurately as shown in the box.

Field	Set of details	Newspaper	Questionnaire	Web
Price	✔	✔	✔	✔
Location	✔	✔	✔	✔
Number of bedrooms	✔	✔	✔	✔
Style/type	✔	✔	✔	✔
Garage	✔	✔	✔	✔
En suite bathroom	✔			✔
Central heating	✔			✔
Double glazing	✔		✔	✔
Garden	✔	✔	✔	✔
Position	✔	✔	✔	✔
Age		✔		
Swimming pool		✔		
Aspect			✔	
Special requirements			✔	

Research results

Looking at all ten fields, I found that a certain number of them were the same on all or some of the sources. I will produce a table to find out the most popular ten fields. These will become the ten for my database. I will put a tick in the box if the field appeared in that source.

Seven fields were chosen from all the sources, one was chosen by three sources and two were chosen by two sources. These are the fields I will use. I will now produce a data capture sheet showing these fields, taken from the information above.

Nick's final product was a database created in Grass (available from Newman College: www.newman.ac.uk). This was used for interrogation purposes to find properties which fall within certain criteria.

Communicating

The second part to the project involved the production of a promotional package for a newly formed company. This included the design of a suitable logo, promotional leaflet, headed notepaper, business card and a folder for the whole package. Again, the project involved research into what is already available so that his final designs can be accurately informed.

An important element to all projects is the choice of software to implement the work. He describes why he has chosen the software for this project as follows:

Software options

I have been asked by Celebration Limited to design a logo for them. I am now going to decide on which drawing package I will use to get the best results for the logo.

There are lots of different drawing packages available to me on my school computer system, all with their good points and bad points. Here is a list of them

- Microsoft Paintbrush
- Microsoft Draw
- PaintShop Pro
- Corel Draw
- Microsoft Word

I am going to use Microsoft Word and Microsoft Paintbrush. I will get the text from Word, then transport it to Paintbrush, and transform it into my logo.

I am very familiar with both of these packages, as I do all of my word-processing on Word, and get most of my graphics from Paintbrush.

Microsoft Word is excellent for text. On our particular version, there are around 100 different fonts, as well as **Bold,** <u>Underline</u>, *Italic* and other styles. There is a Word art option, which has almost an infinite amount of different colours and shapes. You can add shadow or 3D effects and adjust these to almost any angle.

Microsoft Paintbrush will be great for transforming the words into the finished logo. It has a huge colour palette, cut and paste, tools for: freehand, straight lines, squiggly lines, squares, circles, continuous lines, spray paint, text function, paintbrush, eraser, fill colour and select. You can flip, rotate, stretch or skew your image and very importantly, an undo button which goes back three 'moves'. This is much better, for example than Corel Draw, which only goes back one move.

I feel that using both the packages will help me in making the best possible logo.

Nick then designed some logos having looked at others commercially available and tested them on an audience. His initial designs are illustrated in Figure 7.6

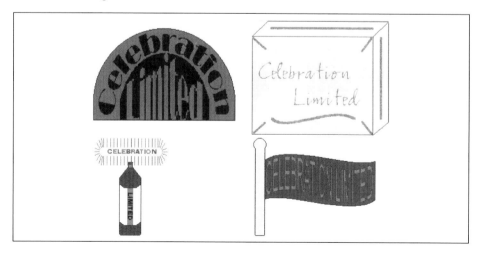

Figure 7.6   Nick's ideas for his logo

Once the research and development was completed, Nick then included the final, approved logo on the business card and the letter heading. Again, the project was sectioned into the same five stages as the previous one.

Pre-set coursework

Some examining boards set part of the coursework themselves, for example, AQA (Assessment and Qualifications Alliance) (www.aqa.org.uk) provides a scenario which has to be analysed by students and a solution has to be provided. The stages of pre-set coursework are the same as other coursework, namely analysis, design, implementation, testing and evaluation. AQA apportions 35 per cent of the 60 per cent coursework mark for this. The other 25 per cent comes through coursework designed by the students through the school.

The new GCSE ICT

The new GCSE ICT, the teaching of which started in September 2001, shows revisions from the old IT course, although the structure of project work remains largely intact. It is a modular course consisting of four modules for the full course and two for the short course (modules 1 and 2 only). The OCR structure is achieved by offering two syllabuses, A and B; one has a more vocational perspective than the other, hence being suitable for a wider audience.

Key issues when choosing a course

If you are thinking about offering GCSE ICT, or looking at the different courses available, the following checklist could be of use.

- Short course or long course? If there are other short courses offered in the school (for example a business studies derivative) then an ICT short course could possibly be combined with it, for coherence.
- Look at the different boards; select a board that offers good guidance and support. There are small differences between the boards.
- Ensure that you have tight control of the project work; use exemplar material on offer from board web sites. You may feel the project work is more tightly specified if you choose a board that pre-sets an element of the coursework.

- Think about the coursework component as being a development of Key Stage 3: there is no reason why it shouldn't start in Year 9. Some schools offer the GCSE short course in Year 9.
- Ensure that there is enough time allocated on the timetable to deliver both theory (assessed by the written exams) and practical (assessed through the coursework). Time allocation is usually insufficient!
- What is the destination of the students? If your school is 11–16 and its students attend a college for their post-16 work, what does the college offer? A GCSE in Information Systems has a computing/programming element which may be more suitable. The new GCSE ICT offers a good foundation for A level and the AVCE as discussed in Chapter 8.
- All of the above rely on the ICT department being able to deliver, monitor and assess the work; specialist ICT staff need to be available. After all, a Geography teacher would not deliver the Maths GCSE! Many schools currently offering GCSE IT are generally finding that the take-up for the course is increasing dramatically. Staffing levels are a key ingredient for good provision.

Summary

The teaching of GUI design issues can provide students with a firm background to the project work involved in the GCSE IT/ICT and this chapter has illustrated how one school includes the GUI dimension as a brief taster through Design and Technology.

GCSE IT and the revised ICT courses being taught for the first time in 2001 represent an important part of Key Stage 4 provision. All exam boards offer a broad range of courses and it should be possible to find one to suit individual school requirements.

There needs to be a clear distinction between the provision for the theory and practical elements of the course. Coursework needs to be monitored with clear deadlines set. It should be remembered that coursework involves much time spent away from the computer through the stages of analysis, design and evaluation and a good GCSE project can have a fairly basic ICT output; as long as the project fits together as a whole. All boards offer help and advice through both telephone contact and their web sites.

Solution to Activity 7.1

The view icon currently being pointed to looks depressed because it refers to the view currently being worked in. It is not immediately obvious that to change the view, a button needs to be pressed and so affordance is not particularly good. The visibility and feedback are quite good because once pressed, the view changes and it can then be related to the graphic image on the icon.

The slider bar has good affordance because it stands proud of the screen and affords to be pressed. When moved (by dragging using the mouse), the page moves down and so visibility is quite good. The feedback is what is in front of you at the end and this is the same document but further down, so it is good because you can clearly see how the window of your text has changed.

CHAPTER 8

Post-16 ICT

The objectives of this chapter are as follows:

- To investigate the structure of A level ICT with particular reference to project work
- To compare the traditional qualifications such as A level with the recently developed AVCE
- To illustrate a practical implementation of the AVCE.

Many schools are still debating whether or not to include ICT as a post-16 subject following on from Year 11 and there are several reasons for this debate: a lack of staffing, a lack of subject knowledge in subject-based ICT studies, and sometimes a reluctance to accept that ICT is a subject in its own right. With the many developments taking place through the move towards the Advanced Vocational Certificate of Education and the mixing and matching possibilities between traditional and vocational qualifications, there is an excellent opportunity for schools to offer post-16 provision with both academic and vocational roots.

In this chapter, I have included details of the structure of post-16 academic and vocational courses, which should be particularly useful for both trainee ICT teachers and schools contemplating which courses to offer.

The background

The post-16 sector of education has changed dramatically since the introduction of vocational qualifications What started off in the mid-1990s as an academic/vocational divide has seen the two different types of qualifications come together as an entry qualification either for work or for university. The introduction of GNVQs has enabled students to become more specialised in a subject rather than taking a range of A levels which may or may not be related. This is quite ironic because GNVQs were developed primarily for entry into employment but a growing number of successful GNVQ students are using them as entry into higher education. The GNVQ at the higher level may prepare students more for what is to come at university through its delivery and assessment structure (which is similar to that in most universities) so it should be no surprise that what have generally been referred to as non-academic qualifications are quite acceptable qualifications for entry to higher education. The Advanced GNVQ is now being replaced by the AVCE.

A level ICT: project work structure

As with the GCSE, the A level includes both taught and project elements. The taught component equates to 60 per cent of the overall mark. All boards offer sample material and in this section, I will discuss the structure of the project work as this is the element of the course where schools have flexibility to encourage students to develop their own systems. With an assessed element like this which is open to interpretation, it is essential that guidance and support can be given by the school at regular times during the project development.

Specifications

The ICT AS and A levels available from the different examining boards all have a common structure: three modules in each year – **Advanced Supplementary (AS)** and A2 (second year A level) – with one module per year devoted to project work worth 40 per cent of the assessment. An important change here is the introduction of the AS level which is assessed at the end of the first post-16 year. Many students would traditionally be free from external exams during this year and the introduction of the AS level has no doubt put an extra strain on students now having exams during three consecutive years (11, 12 and 13).

Apart from the two report projects offered by Edexcel, most of these projects across exam boards have a similar structure with candidates being asked to find suitable problems from external organisations and produce well-documented solutions. In general they require all or most of the following components: specification, analysis, design, implementation, testing, documentation and evaluation and for the student moving on from the GCSE, this will be familiar territory.

The Edexcel examining body
The Edexcel examining body, for example, requires candidates to complete two projects for each of the AS and A2 levels. Although this is a demanding task in the time available, there are some interesting choices. Further details regarding Edexcel can be found on its web site at www.edexcel.org.uk

Edexcel AS projects   The first project involves candidates producing a detailed written report of the ICT administration processes of a major application from one of the areas of industry, commerce, government, society or academia. This complements the systems administration module, giving students the opportunity to investigate a particular application in detail.

Many students rely heavily on relatives or family friends to provide a suitable application from their workplace. Some students, however, have difficulty finding organisations that will help them. In these cases a useful alternative is to investigate the information system at the student's own school.

The second project requires candidates to provide a practical, documented ICT solution to a significant problem that focuses on one of the areas of modelling, communications, modern user interface, multimedia, data logging or database manipulation. This project particularly supports the AS module entitled 'the generation of applications'.

Edexcel A2 projects   The first A2 project consists of a detailed written report of the full range of implications (with stress on the effect on all the people involved) of a major application. This should be taken from one of the same areas as the first project at AS level.

For the second A2 project, students are asked to produce an ICT solution to a significant problem that involves the specification, analysis, design, implementation and evaluation of an application that requires Event-Driven Object Oriented programming. This is an interesting addition to an ICT specification, as it is a topic which is normally more likely to be found in the domain of the Computing syllabus. It does, however, provide students with the opportunity to gain experience of using an Object Oriented Programming language, for example Visual Basic or Delphi.

Other examining bodies

In contrast, for both the AQA and OCR examining bodies, students are obliged to complete just one project each year.

The AS project for AQA requires a solution to a task allowing candidates to demonstrate advanced knowledge of an applications package. The A2 project asks candidates to identify a realistic problem for a real end-user and develop an information system.

The AS project for OCR encourages candidates to demonstrate skills in design, software development, testing and implementation for a specific problem. The A2 project extends candidates further by allowing them to choose a well-defined, user-driven problem which enables them to demonstrate their skills in analysis, design, development, testing, implementation, documentation and evaluation.

What constitutes an AS or A level project?

In general students should select, with guidance from teachers, a problem of sufficient complexity to allow them to demonstrate the necessary skills to meet the criteria for all parts of the project. Take, for example, a database problem where a relational database is selected as the application package. Students should choose a problem where the design needs at least three tables in the relationship. They should implement strict validation techniques and make use of the more advanced features of the package, for example, complex queries and macros. Forms and menus should also be used to customise the user interface.

Choice of software

This is often determined by the resources of the ICT department and the expertise of the teacher.

Staff delivering AS or A level ICT courses for the first time may wish to use reasonably well-tried and tested methods. For example, there have been many successful projects created using database or spreadsheet packages plus there are a number of good books available to support both student and teacher.

Experienced staff may wish to be more adventurous, but it is important to seek guidance from the examination board. Most boards offer specimen project work and training sessions.

Teachers should be encouraged to communicate with other examination centres to discuss ideas and share resources.

Centres following the Edexcel specification, for example, can use the excellent Advanced GCE ICT support network run by teachers. Their web site, on www.hook.ndirect.co.uk/network, offers a valuable source of downloadable teaching materials and useful information.

Choice of problem

There are plenty of opportunities for students tackling a database project. Most students have access to organisations that offer appointments or bookings such as a dental practice, car hire or leisure centre. These all offer suitable models; for example, a dental practice would require at least three entities: patients, appointments and dentists.

Similarly there is no shortage of options for students undertaking spreadsheet projects. Small businesses and retail outlets can provide a rich source of accounting problems, for example, invoicing and sales.

Students should select a problem that requires more than one worksheet and provides a suitable interface to facilitate navigation through the application. They should also make use of many of the advanced features of the package, for example, templates, lookup tables and form controls.

Completing the project

Students should be encouraged to select a real end-user. Often this a requirement of the examination board, but in any case it gives the student a much richer source of information than would be provided from an imaginary user, particularly for the analysis and evaluation stages.

One of the main problems that students encounter is completing the project on time. It is a good strategy to draw up a schedule for the project, setting dates for the completion of each stage. Work can then be submitted on these dates so that progress can be monitored regularly and advice given where necessary. This will also make the eventual assessment of the projects an easier task, as the teacher will already be familiar with the content. It is also wise to set the completion date two weeks ahead of time as insurance against illness or unforeseen problems.

Another common problem is that students spend too much time on implementation thus leaving insufficient time for testing and documentation. To help overcome this problem, students should be made aware of assessment criteria so they can appreciate, for example, that the implementation stage may only be worth a small percentage of the overall mark.

AVCE: structure, implementation and content

The AVCE (often referred to as the vocational A level) is a two-year course and is roughly the equivalent to one A level in single form, and two A levels in double form. This is a particularly exciting post-16 development in that there is now a comparable qualification to A level. The academic/vocational divide which was evident at the start of GNVQ introduction no longer seems to be there.

To gain a single award, students need to study 6 units, increased to 12 for the double award. These consist of a range of compulsory and optional units. Overall, two-thirds of the course is assessed by coursework, one-third by an external assessment which need not be a standard type of exam.

Along with the compulsory units comes a range of optional ones and these are discussed on the Edexcel web site (the board used for the purposes of this discussion).The following case study illustrates how one particular school has implemented the VCE single course.

AVCE: McAuley Catholic High School
The McAuley Catholic High School has a history of Advanced GNVQ provision during the 1990s and has recently introduced the AVCE in both single and double modes. A tool used to help to deliver the course is a school-based web site found at www.mcauleyict.freeserve.co.uk, which includes all assignments, deadlines, specifications and support materials. McAuley offers the Advanced Single VCE, the three compulsory units along with three optional units chosen by the school; to offer a students a choice would be impractical in terms of resourcing and consistency so they carefully match staff expertise to the option modules. Table 8.1 illustrates the modules offered.

Compulsory Units	Optional Units
Unit 1 Presenting information (Portfolio)	Unit 8 Communications and networks (Portfolio)
Unit 2 ICT serving organisations (External)	Unit 13 Managing and developing web sites (External)
Unit 3 Spreadsheet design (Portfolio)	Unit 19 Impact of computers on society and the environment (External)

Figure 8.1   AVCE modules offered at McAuley School

An example of an internally assessed unit
Unit 1 of the compulsory trio is implemented as follows:

Unit 1 Presenting information   In this unit, students have to create documents and gain an understanding of how organisations present and gather information and why specific layouts are used. Table 8.2 shows a tightly structured approach to guidance and advice in completing the unit. Five hours' teaching each week are allocated to the single unit.

Unit 1: Presenting information (Portfolio)

Time Allowed
Advanced ICT VCE Single Award 12 weeks
      Start: 25/09/00 Complete: 21/12/00
Advanced ICT VCE Double Award 6 weeks
      Start: 25/09/00 Complete: 10/11/00

Assessment Evidence to be Produced
• Six original documents created by you for different purposes to show a range of writing and presentational styles. The documents may be in printed form or shown on-screen. They must include one designed to gather information from individuals and one major document of at least three A4 pages.
• A report describing, comparing and evaluating two different standard documents used by each of three different organisations (total of six documents).

Underpinning Knowledge
In completing this assignment, students must demonstrate the development of skills and understanding of knowledge. You should submit many documents before submitting the best quality work. You need to understand about: styles of writing and use of language, accuracy and readability, styles of presentation, how organisations gather and present information. Students must follow 'standard ways of working' covered during the Induction and found on our GNVQ ICT web site www.mcauleyict.freeserve.co.uk

Useful Resources

GNVQ ICT web site www.mcauleyict.freeserve.co.uk Unit 1 resource links and 'standard ways of working'

Thomas Telford Project 40 web site (www.gnvqict.com) some tasks and using some resources

- Documents provided
- Documents collected by students
- Written materials for research
- Look for your own resources

Documentation

Students should keep a planning log of work covered during this assignment. There will be a tick list provided with these support sheets. You need to evaluate your work also at the end of the assignment. You should also keep an error log of any computer problems you encounter during this assignment and how these problems are overcome.

Preparation

Look at the specifications for Unit 1, print these off and follow them carefully. Look at the Assessment section. Look at what you need to do to achieve a grade E, C and A. You should bear these in mind as you work throughout this assignment. Try to aim to achieve the highest possible grade.

Key Skills

Communication C3.1b Make a presentation about a complex subject, using at least **one** image to illustrate complex points

Communication C3.2 Read and synthesise information from **two** extended documents about a complex subject. One of these documents must include at least **one** image

Communication C3.3 Write two different types of documents about complex subjects. One piece of writing should be an extended document and include at least **one** image.

Tasks	Tick when complete	
1. Look at the Thomas Telford Project 40 materials. Work through Assignment 1 but when you get to Activity 2, in pairs collect three examples only of ONE type of document. Work through to Activity 5. Give a presentation to the rest of the group of the characteristics of your type of document, and the strengths and weaknesses of the three documents you looked at. Each pair will be given DIFFERENT types of documents to report on. You must take notes on all of the different types of documents.		
2. Using Thomas Telford materials. Look at Assignment 2 and complete Activities 1 and 2 only. You will have to produce an agenda for a meeting in school and then write up and produce the minutes that you take at the meeting.		
3. Look at the section in the specification headed 'Styles of writing and use of language'. Choose FIVE needs from the first set of bullet points and explain about the writing styles that might be used to complete them. We will go through the whole list and discuss each one.		
4. Look at the section in the specification headed 'Styles of writing and use of language'. Choose THREE examples from the second set of bullet points and explain about the writing styles that might be used. We will go through the whole list and discuss each one.		
5. Read through the section in the specification on 'Accuracy and readability'. Produce a leaflet for GNVQ ICT students on the spellchecker, grammar checker and thesaurus built into Microsoft Word. Include screen grabs and show how to use these tools and the advantages and disadvantages of their use. Use Unit 1 Resources of GNVQ ICT web site to help.		
6. Produce a web page using Microsoft FrontPage to explain about different readability tests. Use Unit 1 Resources of GNVQ ICT web site to help. Print off your		

completed page. Choose a section of text and conduct three different tests on it to see if each test produces the same reading age. Find the reading ages of three different documents of one type. E.g. three newspapers – The Telegraph, The Mirror, The Sun.

7. Produce your own form for joining a club or an organisation, a formal invitation to a party or special event and an email to Edexcel asking for information about the GNVQ ICT course. Include images where appropriate. Use a spellchecker and grammar checker. Also proofread your documents. Use as many 'styles of presentation' features as possible and label them on your printed documents. Check the reading age of your documents. If you need to change them print off an amended version. Write briefly on your document about the styles of writing and use of language chosen.

8. Read through an explanation 'How organisations gather and present information'. Take notes from what is said. A guest speaker might be used here.

9. **Assignment Task** a report describing, comparing and evaluating two different standard documents used by each of three different organisations (total of six documents).

10. **Assignment Task** six original documents created by you for different purposes to show a range of writing and presentational styles. The documents may be in printed form or shown on-screen. They must include one designed to gather information from individuals and one major document of at least three A4 pages.

Table 8.2   AVC Unit 1 Presenting Information

This unit exemplifies the practical nature of the VCE but the production of ICT-based material is not isolated in the use of skills; the material produced is evaluated through the set tasks following the unit specification and this is backed up with discussions and presentations. Each of the ten tasks has to be covered and the final two are given as formal assignments. These receive feedback with an indicative grade from A to E. There is also a generic assessment grid for all units which informs the summative grade for the unit.

As with any internally assessed course, it is essential that students receive formative feedback. Each task is broken into sections and the student receives written comments on the task to date, along with an indicative grade. The student then has a new deadline to improve the work. Students have to demonstrate that they have thoroughly researched and planned each task by keeping a log of their progress. The tutor provides an exemplar template for them which has to be produced and forms part of the assessment. Table 8.3 illustrates how a student should approach the production of this planning evidence.

Advanced Single Award VCE ICT
Unit 1 Planning
Presenting Information

Started work 25/9/00   **Deadline** 21/12/00

Assessment Evidence to be Produced

• Six original documents created for different purposes to show a range of writing and presentational styles. The documents may be in printed form or shown on-screen. They must include one designed to gather information from individuals and one major document of at least three A4 pages.

• A report describing, comparing and evaluating two different standard documents used by each of three different organisations (total of six documents).

Six original documents

To complete this section I need to produce six documents. Each document should include earlier draft copies to show the development of that document. I need to include screen grabs to show spelling and grammar checks, and readability. I need to proofread my documents and use proofreader's marks. I also need to produce a final perfect copy of each document. To get higher grades I need to look at the specifications carefully and make sure I include all necessary features in my documents. For example to get a grade A I need to look at including an index, bullet points, charts and graphs.

The company/organisation/club (*delete as necessary) I have produced documents for is ???

I have tried to create a company identity through my documents. The logo I have produced to add to my documents is:

The reason I chose this logo was ????

The impression I want to create is ???

The documents I have chosen to produce are the following:

Document no.	Type of document	Purpose of document	Software and features used
	Eg sales brochure	What is that document used for?	Eg Publisher for document Paint Shop Pro 7 for the graphics. I used footers, columns, lines, tables, clip art, margins etc.
Document 1			
Document 2			
Document 3			
Document 4			
Document 5			
Document 6			

Six collected documents

To complete this section I need to collect three examples of two types of documents. To get a good grade I need to write a detailed report which looks at each of the two types of documents. I need to describe each document in detail, comment on good and bad points about each document and suggest possible improvements to that document. I need to compare the documents saying which ones I like best/least and give reasons. I must also hand in with my work the collected documents.

The documents I collected were:

Type of document	Examples collected	Good points	Bad points	Suggested improvements
Eg Mobile phone brochures	Eg Nokia	Eg Nice colours and attractive layout	Eg Font too small to read easily in parts	Eg Make small fonts bigger and perhaps choose a different style of font

Log of ICT problems

While working on this unit I encountered the following ICT problems:

No.	ICT problem	How this affected work	How the problem was solved
1	Eg Printer would not print off my work	Eg It held me up and caused frustration	Eg Mr Jones fixed it
2	Eg I lost my floppy disk	Eg It delayed me completing my documents	Eg I bought a box to keep my floppy disks in
3	Eg I did not know how to use Paint Shop Pro 7	Eg It delayed me completing my logo	Eg Mr Hewson showed me how to use Paint Shop Pro 7

Security and Copyright Issues

While working on this unit I encountered the following Security and Copyright Issues:

No.	Security and copyright issue	How issue was resolved
1	Eg If I took pictures and images from the Internet to add to my documents I would be breaking copyright laws	Eg I decided to ask for permission from the company to use the images, or decided to take my own photographs for my documents
2	Eg I thought another student saw my password when I logged into the network	Eg I asked Mr Cole the network manager to allow me to change my password
3	Eg One of the documents I collected was a confidential document	Eg I asked for permission to use it, but when I was told not to use it I decided to find something else

Proofreading

Evidence of proofreading can be found in the first part of this unit where I included early drafts of my six documents which were annotated with proofreaders' marks.

Evaluation

Overall Performance
Overall on this assignment I thought that ???

Good Points
The good points about my work were ???

Bad Points
The bad points about my work were ???

Improvements
If I did this work again I would ???

Table 8.3   Example of a student's template for completing a unit of the AVCE assessment

Although a portfolio module is internally assessed, there are a range of external moderations that take place at the end of the course. All units have to be made available to an appointed external moderator.

Locked into the McAuley programme is the development of **Key Skills**. These skills take the form of Communication, Application of Number and Information Technology as well as Problem Solving and Working with Others and can be gained at different levels. For the purposes of the units offered, the tutor has mapped some elements of Communication and Application of Number to where they occur, as shown in Table 8.4.

Key Skill	Communication				Application of Number					
Criteria ref.	3.1a	3.1b	3.2	3.3	3.1	3.2a	3.2b	3.2c	3.2d	3.3
Unit 1		S	S	K						
Unit 2			K	K						
Unit 3				K	K	K	K	K	K	K
Unit 8	S		K	K						
Unit 13				S						
Unit 19			S							

S = signposting (Key Skills could be included in this unit)

K = keys to attainment (Key Skills are embedded into the assignment)

Table 8.4   Elements of Communication and Application of Number

Activity 8.1
Log onto the Key Skills web site at www.dfee.gov.uk/key/ and have a look at the level 3 criteria for IT and Working with Others. Taking any assessed course that you teach at post-16, map any one of the Key Skills above to your course in the same way as has been done at McAuley.

Assessed Key Skills equate to UCAS (Universities and Colleges Admissions Service) points when applying for a university place so it is always worth integrating them into a course, if possible, as well as teaching them discretely.

The main feature of a portfolio-based course is for the student to provide the appropriate evidence that tasks have been done. These tasks have a standard feedback sheet and are graded so as to equate to the standard A level grading system of A–E and below.

An example of an externally assessed unit
If there was an original lack of parity between vocational/academic courses through their differing assessment structure, then this is certainly not the case now: VCEs have moved away from the 100% coursework assessment without a final or staged exam. Units which are assessed by an external component take the form of a case study given in advance, or a range of questions in the form of an exam. Being a modular course, all assessments are contained within each unit and are not assessed summatively at the end of the two years.

McAuley approaches Unit 2, ICT serving organisations (an externally assessed module) as illustrated in Table 8.5.

Time Allowed
Advanced ICT VCE Double Award   12 weeks
Start: 20/11/00   Complete: 02/03/01 Exam: June 2001

Assessment Evidence to be Produced
A case study analysing a suitable organisation in preparation for the exam in June.

Underpinning Knowledge
In completing this assignment, students must demonstrate an understanding of knowledge. You should produce notes to help

with understanding and revision. You need to understand about: types of organisations, functions within organisations, information and its use and management information systems. Students must follow 'standard ways of working' covered during the Induction and found on our GNVQ ICT web site. www.mcauleyict.freeserve.co.uk

Useful Resources
GNVQ ICT web site (www.mcauleyict.freeserve.co.uk) Unit 2 resource links and 'standard ways of working'

• Written materials for research
• Look for your own resources
• A possible case study from a visit

Documentation
Students should keep a planning log of work covered during this assignment. There will be a tick list provided with these support sheets. You need to evaluate your work also at the end of the assignment. You should also keep an error log of any computer problems you encounter during this assignment and how these problems are overcome.

Preparation
Look at the specifications for Unit 2, print these off and follow them carefully. Look at the Assessment section. Look at what you need to do to achieve a grade E, C and A. You should bear these in mind as you work throughout this assignment. You need to prepare materials and revise to achieve the best possible grade in the June exam.

Key Skills
Communication C3.2 Read and synthesise information from two extended documents about a complex subject. One of these documents should include at least **one** image.

Communication C3.3 Write two different types of documents about complex subjects. One piece of writing should be an extended document and include at least **one** image.

Tasks	Tick when complete	
1. Look at textbooks to make notes on what an organisation is and common features. Look at different types of organisations: multinational companies, commercial organisations, industrial organisations, public service organisations, banks and building societies, and utility companies.		
2. Look at types of information in organisations, make notes on these. These include: customers and clients; managers and employees, manufacturing, suppliers; wholesalers and retailers and distribution. You will research one of these to give a presentation to the rest of the group.		
3. Look at functions within organisations: internal and external functions.		
4. Look at organisational structures: hierarchical or tall structure, flat structure. Research one commercial, one manufacturing and one public service organisation. Draw an organisational chart for each. You will need to find out about functions and departments to be able to do this. Comment on the background of each organisation, number of branches, turnover and anything else they do besides their main aim.		
5. Look at information flow diagrams and try to draw two for the organisations you have researched above. To do this you need to look at methods for communicating information: verbal and documents. Look at ICT systems that are used: EDI or e-commerce, LAN or Internet for email, telephone, fax and centralised database systems.		
6. At this point we will try to arrange a visit or a guest speaker to look at a real case study.		
7. Make notes on Management Information Systems; write about MIS for a researched organisation.		

Table 8.5   AVCE Unit 2 ICT Serving Organisations (External)

The module is geared around a final externally assessed piece of work which consists of a range of questions based on a particular case study scenario. Students undertake a mock exam from the exemplary case study on the web.

The McAuley web site is a useful resource for AVCE and is well worth a look.

Summary

In this chapter, I have discussed the structure of A level and the AVCE ICT with particular regard to the issues involved in project work (with the A level) and one school's approach (with the AVCE). Both types of courses encourage students to look at live situations outside of the school.

Post-16 ICT has broadened considerably with the introduction of the AVCE and the academic/vocational divide seems to have disappeared with the option of matching AVCE with traditional A level subjects.

It should be remembered that there is still a large theoretical element to post-16 courses, particularly A level courses, and this cannot be delivered through project work. Time needs to be put aside for the academic element as it constitutes 60 per cent of a course. Good textbooks need investigating as well as vast web resources. A starting point for textbooks could be the Heathcote series; details are available at www.payne-gallway.co.uk. Also, a good web resource for teaching material relevant to all post-16 ICT teaching is www.histman.demon.co.uk

The use of the Internet in education

The objectives of this chapter are as follows:

- To discuss the structure and usage of electronic communication in education through email and computer conferencing
- To investigate some specific uses of the web in education.

As with other chapters, the objectives are achieved through investigating work in schools.

The Internet is having a major influence on the way we access information and communicate with each other. As themed throughout this book, this chapter provides live examples of how the Internet can provide a useful resource to us all. This is one element of new technology that is probably familiar to you, either through personal use of email and web searching, or use within your subject area.

What is the Internet?

The Internet is a network of networks where potentially millions of computers can communicate with each other. The Internet consists of the physical elements involved in the communications process. Your school will connect to the Internet through an **Internet Service Provider** (ISP), possible through the LEA, Research Machines Limited (RML) or another source. To connect to an ISP, your school will probably use a dial-up connection and this may be in integrated services digital network (ISDN) form. Digital transfer is quicker and more efficient than a standard analogue connection. You may also connect through the new asymmetric digital subscriber line that is being installed in exchanges throughout the UK. This allows a much higher connection speed and also promotes the idea of the 'always on' type of Internet connection.

There are many parts to the Internet including the main electronic information provider known as the **World Wide Web (WWW)**. Lots of information is stored on computers all over the world and this is available to all through the web: the web is a facility offered through the Internet, as is email, an electronic communication facility available from one person to another person, both using computers. So you can see the hierarchy of services underneath the Internet at the root of the tree. So how can these facilities benefit education? Well, you have seen some through the examples within MFL in Chapter 5, an obvious use of an international facility, but there are others.

Electronic communication through email

You probably have access to email at home through your own ISP and so can relate this experience to possible use in school. Teachers are beginning to do this as illustrated in the case study.

Email: the Manton School
Peter, an English teacher at the Manton School, has gradually become involved in using ICT in English through his personal use of email. He involves students of all years in email communication and this has been recognised by the ICT coordinator. Peter now teaches elements of electronic communication as part of an ICT awareness programme in Year 9. All students study the GCSE short course at Key Stage 4, and this prepares them for many elements of it. It is also an indicator that some elements of GCSE ICT can be introduced and taught throughout other curriculum subjects. He discusses his use of ICT as follows:

> It happened by accident really.... I have been an email user for about four years and decided that since most of my English students had access to email, I would include it as a discussion point for a class debate. This was good because it highlighted the different approaches the children have towards it... the one line communication, the one letter word. We discussed the issues involved in sending me an email with an excuse for not handing in homework... issues like being able to plan for an excuse and not

being put on the spot, me being in a position to give a considered response... this was a part of it which led on to what type of email software used, how replies are sent, how messages are stored and this led me to find out more about it myself, hence a few timetabled sessions through ICT in Year 9. All of our students have a school email address so it is reasonable for me to include email exercises in English. This is to do with exchanging ideas about discussion issues prior to the discussion taking place.

Peter illustrates how his own experiences can be the starting point for use within a subject. There are many issues related to electronic communication which differ from other forms of communication and the following have been touched on by Peter.

Email is asynchronous
It is realistic to compare email with writing a letter and sending it though the post: an email is composed, sent and replied to. Communication is only one way at any moment in time. Responses to emails tend to be quicker than responses to a letter but responding can involve thought and reflection. This is in contrast to a discussion between two people or a telephone conversation where communication can be in both directions, i.e. synchronous. Email communication can be further enhanced with the possibility of sending the same email to a group of recipients simultaneously, using mailing lists.

Email has a written culture
When emailing messages, people sometimes miss out capitals and grammar and abbreviate as much as possible. There is an immediacy about email that has become acceptable, even if not desirable. Also, when two people are communicating through email, the number of emails between them tends to be more than if they were, say, writing letters. You can attach files to emails which have been created in another application.

Email has a global capacity
It does not matter where an email recipient lives; once you are connected to the Internet, distance is irrelevant; you just send the message.

Activity 9.1
Think about email and possible links with your subject:
* How can you encourage students to work autonomously using email?
* List the ways you can benefit from email.

How do we get access to email?

Many schools now have access to email through their own ISP along with the other Internet facilities such as the web. These are often provided by the LEA or nationally known companies who provide good backup facilities. You can see where your email facility comes from by looking at the structure of an individual email account. For example, raynerm@davenant. essex.sch.uk is the email address of Mark Rayner, the Head of ICT at Davenant Foundation School in Essex. All members of staff at Davenant have their email addresses in the form of surname[,] initial@Davenant.essex.sch.uk and the specific school name is substituted with other schools across Essex. There are other email structures around, for example, my own is T.Russell@mdx.ac.uk; mdx identifies the institution, ac refers to an academic one and uk locates the country. Other countries are quite easy to recognise, for example nl – Netherlands, au – Australia.

Activity 9.2
If you are already an email user, think about the way you treat email. For example, do you read email regularly? Do you respond to all emails? How do you organise your emails? List the things that form part of your own email awareness when you use it.

Email: Sandringham School
At Sandringham, the ICT department has developed a role-play situation where Year 8 students take part in an assembly and become involved in a discussion about the use of email versus snail mail (i.e. writing letters). Table 9.1 illustrates this.
When using email in school, it is essential that the issues are discussed

Year 8 assembly

Email

Scene:
Two people sit at a desk – one is typing onto a laptop, the other writing onto paper.
Props: Laptop
Paper
Envelope
Stamp
Scene change cards
Bell

The aims:
To show the benefits of email over snail mail. The correct usage of email and the netiquette of email. This will cover the email etiquette that will be the main focus of the classroom activities.
Round one:
Email or snail mail?

RIC: What *are* you doing?
STB: Writing to my friend in Australia.
RIC: So am I!
STB: I'm using email, it's much quicker than your snail mail.
RIC: Oh yeah, I'll race you then. Your email against my letter.
STB: OK then, are you ready? Right, GO!
          Funny frantic typing and writing bit.
RIC: There finished! Told you writing was quicker!
STB: My email reached Australia while you were still licking the stamp!

Round one to email!
Round two:
Junk mail…

RIC: I can't believe it! I've just opened all my post today and nearly all of it is complete rubbish. It's junk! Look at this... *Reads letter...*
Dear Mr Camill (They can't even spell my name right) Congratulations, you have been selected by our computer and stand to win a grand prize of a new Vauxhall Corsa or a set of hand crafted salt and pepper pots. Just complete the form below and return it with your first order of over £50 and we guarantee you one of the above prizes! What have you got to lose?
I wish there were some way of stopping these people sending me such rubbish!

STB: Well with email you can stop undesirable email reaching your computer. So I get very little junk mail these days.

RIC: Bah! You win again!

Round two to email!

Round three:
Where in the world?

RIC: It's all very well having this email but I'm never in the same place, I move around, I keep ahead of the game, I'm a wanderer, a ducker, a diver, a wheeler, a dealer... I can't keep coming back to the same computer every time I want to send a message. With this, envelope and stamp I can send a message from anywhere.

STB: Anywhere?

RIC: Anywhere, well anywhere with a post-box and a decent postal system!

STB: Ah, well, with email you can send a message from anywhere in the world, as long as you have an Internet connection. That could even be a laptop and a mobile phone!

RIC: So I could send a message from the middle of the Sahara Desert then?

STB: Yes.

RIC: Doh! You win again!

Round three to email!

Round four:

Where do I start?

RIC: OK, OK, OK you win. I want email, I want email NOW!

STB: Well you can, everyone in the school will be given their OWN email address! This means that students will be able to communicate with friends, relatives and the world of business all from their user area!

RIC: Excellent, I want to tell everyone my address then I can get lots of mail and be really popular!

STB: Not so fast, just like your password you have to be careful who you give your address to. You wouldn't tell every one your home address would you?   Or your telephone number?

RIC: Well, no I don't think I would.

STB: I think there are a few things you need to be told before you can be allowed anywhere near an email account.

RIC: OK then, fire away.

STB: I've asked some friends to help me. Who has number one?

Each point is given to various members of the year team.

No.1   **Never give your email address to a stranger**

STB: You can never be sure what they will do with it. Next, number two…

No.2   **Don't give someone else's email address away.**

STB: You wouldn't give their phone number away, would you? Number three…

No.3   **Don't say anything in an email that you wouldn't want anyone to say to you.**

STB: Don't use email as a way of sending abuse to someone. Number four…

No.4	**Tell a member of IT if you receive any email that you do not like.**
STB:	They can help you to stop it happening again. Number five…
No.5	**Don't use anybody else's email address without them knowing.**
STB:	If the address isn't yours then you have no business using it.
RIC:	Right, I think I've got it now. Just one more thing.
STB:	What's that?
RIC:	(Turning laptop over in his hands) Where do I stick the stamp on this thing?
The end	

Table 9.1   Email versus snail mail at Sandringham School

and the Sandringham approach shows that ICT does not always involve students sitting in front of computers. Issues of security as discussed at Sandringham are important. It is possible to transmit viruses through email, through using attachments. Two well-known cases of virus transmission in this way are the Melissa and the 'I love you' viruses. These spread by email users opening attachments sent to them which take the reader's address book and then send the virus on again to everyone in the address book. Some email programs automatically open attachments so it is important that your school uses one which does not do this. Also, it is important to have a virus checker installed on computers so that problems like this can be detected.

Computer conferencing

So far, we have discussed the use of email in both personal and professional situations; another means of electronic communication is the computer conference.

Computer conferencing facilities differs from email in one particular way: rather than sending an individual message to a recipient, you post a message to a predefined location (known as a conference) and it is the responsibility of the members of that group to read it. An analogy for this is the use of the bulletin board in the staff room.

The Yahoo! Groups (http://groups.yahoo.com) facility can be useful because of its web-based location; by this, it means that being on the web, it can be accessed from any computer that is linked and does not involve logging on to a specific ISP.

A conference usually has a coordinator for administration purposes and there is usually something in common between the people taking part in the conference. It is usually the responsibility of the conference coordinator to sign up and delete people from the conference at appropriate times.

Yahoo! Groups conference: Willowfield School

A Yahoo! Groups conference has been set up by the Head of ICT at Willowfield School for use within her department. The three folders illustrated contain the following material:

- Folder 1: shared teaching material
- Folder 2: minutes of departmental meetings
- Folder 3: weekly notices

Members of the department have the responsibility of reading the conference on a weekly basis as the head of department has a policy of not producing printed material unless it is absolutely necessary: if a colleague wants printed output then it is their responsibility to get it. Folder 1 has sub-folders in it, where the teaching material is broken down into year groups. Within each year group, there are further sub-folders on topics, for example, project 1, Excel, hardware. Each of these sub-folders contain a range of prepared overheads and handouts.

Designing a group conference

When you set up a conference using a facility like this, it is important that it has been designed in the first place. The structure discussed in the case study was designed on paper and is illustrated in Figure 9.1.

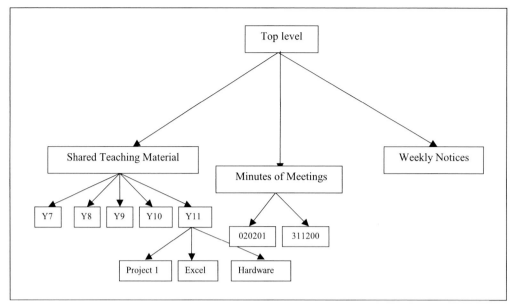

Figure 9.1   Structure of the Yahoo! Groups conference at Willowfield School

Implementing the design resulted in the practical illustration of Yahoo! Groups in Figure 9.2.

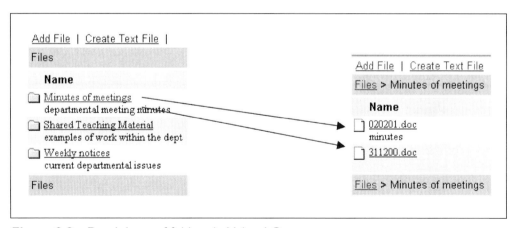

Figure 9.2   Breakdown of folders in Yahoo! Groups

Activity 9.3
Think about the setting up of a conference using Yahoo! Groups for use by members of your department.
• Design the overall file structure that you think would be useful.
• Have a go at setting up the conference by following the instructions at the Yahoo! Groups home page. Sign up members of your department.

The World Wide Web

The World Wide Web has received much publicity since the UK general election in 1997. There is a central government commitment to ensure that all schools and libraries are on-line by 2002 and that they are using the technology to enhance teaching and learning. Many secondary schools are already doing this, of course, and there is every reason to believe that the stated government objective is achievable. Many schools now have large ICT resourcing, intranets, access to email for staff and students and much more. We need look no further than recent developments in web access in the home to see how this is achievable: ISPs offering a free service, local dial-up facilities and several incentives to change telephone service providers to companies who offer free web access (including the cost of the telephone call) at off-peak times.

How are web sites created?

Producing web pages to form a web site originally had to be done in **hypertext markup language (HTML)** but now this isn't necessary. There are many software products on the market that will do this for you and this releases the web designer to the designing process without having to be involved in the writing of computer code to achieve the desired results. The software used still has to be mastered, of course, but it is much easier than it used to be. In its simplest form, it is possible to create a web page from within Word or Publisher but it is sound advice to use a product specifically produced for web page production (usually referred to as web authoring). Dreamweaver comes to mind as it is frequently used in schools and can be investigated on the web at www.macromedia.com

A starting point

Along with the initiatives of the government in 1997 came the launch of the **Virtual Teachers Centre (VTC)**, a resource base which will certainly contain material suitable for you. This is a part of the National Grid for Learning, which forms the backbone of the on-line communications thrust in education.

Activity 9.4

Identify an area of professional development of interest to you and attempt to find a web site of use through the VTC (http://vtc.ngfl.gov.uk). List the resources made available through the site and follow some of them up. Explore the site.

To use the web as a resource involves a little work and this can centre around the use of searching techniques. The case study at Aylward School illustrates the use of the web as a tailored resource in art education. (This is an edited version of an article by Rebecca Sinker (2001).)

Using the web in Art education: Aylward School

Digital photography has enabled many Art departments to broaden their work and easily integrate ICT into the production and editing of images. But in the field of art education, there are other ways to bring the subject to life without having to visit museums or art galleries; the web can be a huge resource (as in any subject) but key to any resource is having it focused and tailored to the desired audience.

Aylward School have taken part in a research project in Art education which has added new dimensions to the way art is perceived by students. The DARE (Digital Art Resource for Education) project has enabled teachers to access digital arts and plan work for a range of age groups, bringing the subject to life for students and more importantly, informing their work. The project has shown the need for teachers and students to engage critically with the Internet as a distance learning tool and shown how new technology can support art and design. The project is a collaboration between Middlesex University and the Institute of International Visual Arts, with funding from the Arts Council of England.

The project has involved the use of the web to alleviate the problem that students and teachers are frequently not able to access the products and debates of contemporary visual art. The project uses the web as a medium for discourse and publication as well as research. Students can evaluate and contribute to the resource through dialogue and creative participation, using email, discussion forums and creating their own web pages. In short, it is a free, flexible interactive resource base intended as a support and development mechanism. The home page for the site is at www.dareonline.org

The use of DARE with Year 12 A level Art and Photography
An Art teacher at Aylward decided to try the resource with his Year 12 A level Art and Photography students. He had already introduced students to the work of Christian Boltanski and, following initial discussions, he set them the task of looking through the site to see what ideas they could come up with in relation to one of DARE's themes, Absence and Presence. They gradually built up a picture of the work of Boltanski and other artists, while developing their own ideas. One student, Monique, investigated the idea of missing persons through Boltanski's use of photographs of Holocaust victims and later through the social practice in the USA of publicising missing children on the side of milk cartons. She published her work on the web through the DARE site (Figure 9.3).

The DARE resource has clearly influenced the work of Monique and other students. Their work has been exhibited publicly as well as being published on the web. One student commented:

> One good thing about the DARE site is just having people's work on it and having our work on it as well, for people around the world to see, to get feedback from them.

This web resource has also been used in Year 9. The head of Art used the site for her own resources in the planning stage of a project on cultural identities and diaspora. Although she had material from before, the site gave her new ideas which ultimately updated her work. The web has much to offer teachers in the planning stage of a project.

The Art department at Aylward has always focused on contemporary art but short of taking students out of school, viewing contemporary works has always been difficult. The web has made this much more accessible. There is no doubt that using the DARE resource, and all the sites that have been set up as links, introduces the students and the teachers to

Monique Nelson's Web Page

My initial research focused on memorials and remembrance because Christian Boltanski once said he believed his works are memorials.

Boltanski's illuminated arches resembled the traditional ones used in Renaissance art. My final composition was influenced by this.

In America, milk cartons are used to appeal for information about missing children. Boltanski's photos on old, rusted tins reminded me of this, and also inspired me to try it myself on glass milk bottles.

One of my designs for the bottles' composition was to have them coming down a free-standing spiral.

This is one of the finished bottles with my image on it.

The final display of the bottles is in a pyramid shape, with the image gradually disappearing from the surface.

Figure 9.3 Monique Nelson's web page

work by artists who they had previously never encountered and who they would have been unable to find through existing resources within the school. DARE has provided the front end to a broader curriculum.

There are some general issues related to displaying material on the web which are relevant to all subject areas; for example, the quality of the reproduction whether it be photographs or other types of image. Art is a subject where images are most important and it can be seen from the web site that production is better than many secondary sources such as photocopies. The important issue is that students are able to use the web in a way *they* select and not within a framework structured totally by the teacher.

The immediacy of the web with quick results is an important feature that several students commented on:

It was good for a starting point and then we got our own ideas and we developed those.

> If you've never heard of a particular artist before, and then you see their work on the web site, if you like the way it looks on the web site, you might want to actually see what it looks like in real life, so it'll push you to go out and find the work.

Gallery visits ideally form an integral part of art education and the web pages on Boltanski provided some ideas prior to a visit, as mentioned by the Art teacher:

> They went to the Tate Modern recently and saw Christian Boltanski and Doris Salcedo's work and made the connection with what they'd seen previously on the Web site ... two students came back and said 'Oh Bill Viola's at the Tate Modern' and hearing kids get excited about that ... talk about all these artists is great, it's exactly what you want, isn't it, it's a springboard

He also felt that it had opened his students up to the possibilities of working in different media and showing work in other ways.

> One student is doing a video installation now using two or three monitors that she just wouldn't have done before ... being aware of time-based art, rather than pictorial or paper-based. It's given them a wider perspective.

Issues for discussion regarding DARE

These issues are generic in that they may apply to any subject where an exhibition plays an important part. Regarding Art education, students and teachers discussed the following:

- Who is the audience for students' work when published globally?
- Can you engage in a dialogue with that audience?
- Can you exhibit your examinable (in this case A level) exhibition on the web?
- Can the web enable an extension of the debate about presented work beyond the school?

The final point relates to the discussion group element to the web. Discussion groups are not new and are available through many web sites. For example, the Virtual Teachers Centre has themed discussions. Yahoo!

Groups have been discussed earlier in this chapter and can also be used as a discussion group.

The DARE project illustrates the use of the web as a tailored resource where the focus is a critical engagement with both the subject and the medium illustrating how learning and teaching can take on a new dimension. The use within Art education has been focused to improve the learning experience. This resource-based approach is a good, timeless use of the web and can act as a major integrating factor of the use of ICT within a subject.

An alternative to searching the web is going directly to a site through its URL, i.e. its unique web address home page. The DARE project illustrated this through using the home page as a gateway to further site access. Many web sites have been kite-marked by the NGfL, which suggests that they contain worthwhile material.

Key to using the web as a resource bank is being able to acquire the information you want, when you want it. A general search using a search engine can easily produce 1 million hits, i.e. web sites which have satisfied the search criteria entered. It is unlikely that all these sites will be useful and so it is important to narrow down the search as much as possible. For example, using the Google search engine (www.google.com), I wanted to find out about sites which would update my understanding of the numeracy strategy, particularly as it is now affecting secondary schools. By using the search criteria *"numeracy strategy"*, I came up with site references to only the numeracy strategy because the Google search engine identifies sites that contain *both* words and not either, if you include within quotation marks. It is worth looking at the help pages for each of the search engines. Searching the web is much underrated and it is important to work out an efficient strategy for using a range of search engines.

Summary

This chapter has focused on the important issues of using electronic communication in education. Email and computer conferencing have been discussed and both types of facilities are freely available. Being generic in nature, both can be used as an effective tool across all subjects and can also be used for professional development.

The web is a huge resource and used in a tailored way can support all subjects but it is important that web resources are used critically as there is no quality control involved in setting up web pages. Using web resources which are kite-marked by the NGfL is a good starting point for broader investigations.

Solutions to activities

Activity 9.1

First, by ensuring that all students have a school-based email account, you can encourage electronic discussion between them. They could be given a group working exercise which involves them exchanging ideas in order to solve a specified problem. The electronic element can be done during their free time or at a computer club. Many schools now expect students to use ICT in non-teaching time and once set up, students soon develop an autonomous approach to their work. Of course, this needs careful monitoring!

Second, you can exchange files through attachments, keep in contact over a period of absence. By using the facility to send to multiple users, you can communicate with everyone in a particular group, for example in the same department, the same year group form teachers, the members of a working party. You can distribute minutes of meetings without using printed form.

Activity 9.2

There are no right or wrong answers to this. The way you deal with email will probably involve you thinking about some of the following:

- The way you write messages. Do you stick to standard grammar or do you abbreviate when you can? Either way, you are probably consistent.
- How often do you read your email? If you give your email address to others, you should read it at least twice each week.
- Do you make reference to **netiquette**, that is, the use of smiling faces, the use of capitals if you want to shout.
- When you reply to a message, do you reply to all parties in the address list or just to the sender? There are times when you should do one or the other depending on who you want to read the reply.
- Do you have folders in your emailing software so that you can group messages together? If you have a filtering system, messages can automatically be sent to a relevant folder. This can make the emailing setup look much tidier than just having incoming messages being listed together.

- When composing messages, do you do it on-line or off-line? It is cheaper to compose messages while you are not on-line and queue them for sending once you log on.
- Is it necessary to respond to all emails? It may not be, so don't feel that you have to.

Reference

Sinker, R. (2001) 'Distance no object: developing DARE, the Digital Art Resource for Education', *International Journal of Art and Design Education* 20(1), 31–40.

Appendix: Glossary of terms

This glossary lists the acronyms and terms used throughout this book in the context of ICT in education. Where appropriate, explanations are given. Further details of agencies included can be found at www.dfes.gov.uk/links.shtml. Also, you will find an excellent on-line dictionary of computing and ICT terms at InstantWeb www.instantweb.com/D/dictionary/

Advanced (A) level: taken after two years of study, the second year follows the AS level year. A level ICT has 40 per cent coursework and 60 per cent exam.

Advanced interactive video (AIV)

Advanced Supplementary (AS) level: a qualification in its own right, awarded after one year of study, usually at the end of Year 11. Further study the following year can result in a full *A level*.

Advanced Vocational Certificate of Education (AVCE): a new post-16 qualification that can be taken in single or double mode. Otherwise known as the vocational A level.

Affordance: an icon is said to have affordance if it is obvious what to do with it from its appearance. For example, many icons appear in 3D form, suggesting that they should be pressed. In such cases, there is a visual clue as to what to do; this illustrates good affordance. This is closely linked to *feedback* and *visibility*.

Assessment and Qualifications Alliance (AQA) examining board

Asymmetric digital subscriber line (ADSL): a digital telephone line which gives fast access to on-line resources through its large bandwidth.

Attainment Targets (ATs): the statements within each National Curriculum document that describe what is expected from students at the end of each Key Stage. In ICT, there is one attainment target and along with this come eight progressive *level descriptions* and one describing exceptional performance.

Beginners' All-Purpose Symbolic Instruction Code (BASIC): a computer programming language used in education mainly during the 1980s and early 1990s.

Bit mapped (bmp): a format for saving images which corresponds directly to how they are displayed on the screen.

Branching database: a database that, when designed, can be looked at in a hierarchical, tree-like way. Each element can have several other elements sprouting down from it.

British Educational Communications and Technology Agency (BECTA): the agency with responsibility for developing the use of ICT in education through both its resource base and various funded initiatives.

Career Entry Profile (CEP): a document that *newly qualified teachers* (NQTs) take into their first job illustrating their strengths and weaknesses. The CEP forms the basis of a contract between the NQT and the school for staff development purposes.

Centre for Information on Language Teaching and Research (CILT) (Stirling)

Compact disc read only memory (CD-ROM): a CD which can be accessed but not modified. These have a lot of storage space (about 700 mb) and a fast access time.

Computer Aided Learning (CAL) package: the use of a software application for a specific educational purpose; for example, a program to develop numeracy skills.

Department for Education and Employment (DfEE)

Department for Education and Skills (DfES): this is the renamed DfEE. Its brief has changed slightly but it is still the governing body for education.

Desktop publishing (DTP): software to facilitate laying out a document in a form suitable for professional printing.

Digital Art Resource for Education (DARE)

Electronic mail (email)

Feedback: closely linked to *affordance* and *visibility*. Feedback refers to the information sent back to the user once an action within a *GUI* is completed. For example, the feedback when dragging a slider bar in a word-processing application usually results in the window changing. If the information sent back is obvious, then feedback is good.

General Certificate of Secondary Education (GCSE): an external assessment usually taken in Year 11. GCSE ICT has 60 per cent coursework and 40 per cent exam.

General National Vocational Qualification (GNVQ): this external assessment is different from the GCSE in that it has a vocational focus. It can be taken at three levels: foundation, intermediate and advanced – the last of which is equivalent in standard to *A level.*

General Professional Studies (GPS): the generic component of a *PGCE* which deals with issues of relevance to trainees from all subject areas.

Generic software elements: a standard range of facilities contained in software packages of a similar kind. For example, all word processors have a cut-and-paste facility; all spreadsheets have a fill down/copy cells facility.

Graphic User Interface (GUI): (pronounced gooey) this interface can be interacted using a mouse or the like. The interface has icons which have to be clicked on to achieve the desired results. The icons are usually in the form of a metaphor, for example, a top-level GUI is called a desktop and is usually a Windows derivative.

Head of department (HOD)

Higher education institution (HEI)/school partnership: the relationship between the training provider (the HEI) and a school involved in teaching practice. This involves payment to schools for supervision and mentoring.

Human–computer interaction (HCI): the study of the communication issues related to humans and computers.

Hypertext markup language (HTML): a computer programming language used to create web pages.

ICT coordinator: the teacher responsible for ICT throughout the school. This may or may not be the head of ICT.

Information and Communication Technology (ICT): recently renamed from *IT* to incorporate a broader definition through many technological developments.

Information Technology (IT): this subject has been renamed Information and Communication Technology (ICT), although it still exists in some form, for example, as a university subject (however, this will probably change).

Initial Teacher Training (ITT)

Integrated package: a software application which includes elements which can share data. An example of this is Microsoft Office, which has a spreadsheet, word processor, database and a presentation application where information saved in one can be used in all the others.

Integrated services digital network (ISDN): a digital communication technology which may replace the standard telephone connection. It is faster through the use of fibre-optic wire.

Interactive video (IV)

Internet Service Provider (ISP): this is a company (for example, Tesco, Freeserve) which provides you with access to the Internet. It is usually free but if used from home, you will incur telephone charges either pro-rata or through a flat monthly charge.

Key Skills: these are specific subjects which can be taught discretely or integrated within other subjects. Information Technology, Application of Number, Communication, Problem Solving and Working with Others are the main ones.

Key Stage (KS)

Level descriptions: these are progressive descriptions of how a student is working within one of eight levels (+ exceptional performance) within a National Curriculum subject. It is statutory to report a level at the end of Key Stage 3 and this should be backed up with evidence.

Local education authority (LEA)

Modern Foreign Languages (MFL)

Monitoring, assessment, recording and reporting (MARR): the term used for giving students feedback on their work both formatively and summatively. This includes reporting progress to parents.

Multiple integration: I have used this term to refer to a method of using ICT in schools where curriculum areas other than ICT use ICT within their subject and also involve other departments. For example, the development of a DTP application beginning in English and passing over to Art for the design elements. English, Art and possibly an ICT teacher are involved in the process.

National Council for Educational Technology (NCET): this has now been replaced by *BECTA.*

National Grid for Learning (NGfL): a web-based resource to promote lifelong learning. It consists of more than 300,000 pages and continues to grow.

Netiquette: a code of conduct which should be adhered to when using the web. Politeness should prevail. For example, do not send an email to all the people in a group if it isn't necessary.

Newly qualified teacher (NQT): see also *Career Entry Profile.*

New Opportunities Fund (NOF): £230 million of funding was made available through the National Lottery to support ICT training for teachers. Training providers had to provide training to improve the use of ICT in delivering the curriculum in the classroom through focused curriculum initiatives.

Office for Standards in Education (OFSTED): the inspection agency responsible for reporting on institutional delivery of statutory requirements in schools, colleges and teacher training establishments.

Oxford, Cambridge and Royal Society of Arts (OCR) examining board

Personal computer (PC)

Postgraduate Certificate of Education (PGCE)

Qualifications and Curriculum Authority (QCA): the authority responsible for kite-marking qualifications and developing material to support the implementation of the National Curriculum.

Qualified Teacher Status (QTS): this is an award of competence following a programme of teacher training. To be awarded QTS, trainees need to demonstrate that they have achieved all of the teaching competencies as well as passing the three skills tests of Numeracy, Literacy and ICT.

Questioning techniques: the techniques used to interrogate a database or a search on the web. These will vary according to the software used.

Random-access memory (RAM): volatile computer memory, i.e. the contents are lost once the computer is switched off.

Second year A level (A2)

Single integration: I have used this term to refer to a method of using ICT in schools where curriculum areas other than ICT use ICT within their subjects but do not involve work within other subject areas. Integration is restricted to curriculum areas in a self contained manner with little or no input from others.

Special educational needs (SEN)

Special educational needs coordinator (SENCO)

Teacher Training Agency (TTA): the managing body for teacher training.

Uniform resource location (URL): a unique address for a web page.

Virtual Teachers Centre (VTC): a web-based resource which teachers can access in order to share ideas through discussion groups and look at a range of freely available teaching material.

Visibility: this is linked to *affordance* and *feedback*. Visibility refers to the effect of an action within a GUI, for example, when clicking on an icon, is it immediately obvious what has happened? An example of good visibility is clicking on a 3D icon and seeing it become depressed; the action has created a recognisable effect.

Vocational Certificate of Education (VCE): see also *AVCE*.

What You See Is What You Get (WYSIWYG): this refers to a document that looks the same on the screen as it does when printed out.

World Wide Web (WWW): a service offered through the Internet which links information (in the form of pages) available on the computers linked to the Internet.

Index